DEVON
TALES OF MY
AND MURDER

C000002427

DEVON
TALES OF MYSTERY
AND MURDER

Judy Chard

COUNTRYSIDE BOOKS
Newbury, Berkshire

COUNTRYSIDE BOOKS
3 Catherine Road
Newbury, Berkshire

To view our complete range of books,
please visit us at
www.countrysidebooks.co.uk

ISBN 1 85306 717 2

Designed by Mon Mohan

Produced through MRM Associates Ltd., Reading
Printed by J. W. Arrowsmith Ltd., Bristol

Contents

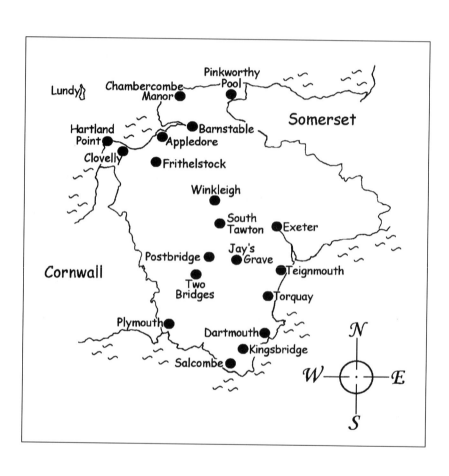

Foreword

'Something old, something new . . .' so the saying goes, and you will find both inside the covers of this book. There are ghosts and wreckers, and strange tales of haunted places, as well as the modern stories such as Donald Crowhurst's doomed voyage and the Luxton family tragedy. The 'old' stories have been updated as I have done more research and talked to more people – a new angle, a new approach. The many years I spent both broadcasting and travelling the leafy lanes of Devon to remote village halls, the dreaded after luncheon or dinner talk in a posh hotel or town hall taught me that as the song says, 'It ain't what you do, it's the way that you do it' and over and over again when I was asked to speak I was assured they wanted to hear the old favourites as well as the new ones. I am grateful to such people as Bossiney, Obelisk and Orchard; to Old Uncle Tom Cobleigh an' all whose ghosts appear occasionally among the pages – showing me what is always popular. Theo Brown, considered one of the best of this type of historian in the county, is one to whom I am much indebted since I started my non-fiction writing career. And particular thanks are also due to *Devon Life* for their support and co-operation.

A final big thank you must also go to Nick Wotton for his specially written poem and some of the photographs – most of all for acting as driver to the distant parts of his beloved Dartmoor.

Enjoy your reading!

Judy Chard

SOMETHING OUT OF HELL

THE three young men had been to Evensong in a church in the prestigious area of the Warberries in Torquay, South Devon. Little could they have imagined after the calm mood of the service they had just attended, how the next few hours would hold such horror that one of them would later describe it as 'something out of hell'.

The well known novelist and magazine writer Beverley Nichols, his brother and a young friend, Lord St Audries, were spending a few days in this then exclusive watering place favoured by the rich and elderly. It was a warm evening and they decided to wander slowly up Middle Warberry Road admiring the large houses built both sides of the street. Much to their surprise they came upon a derelict house, whose broken gate held the name 'Castel-a-Mare'.

'Come on chaps, let's explore,' Nichols had the natural curiosity of a writer.

The other two, on their way to visit friends, hung back for a moment, but they saw how keen Nichols was, and were now somewhat intrigued themselves by the fearful looking, dilapidated and empty house with its glassless windows. They followed him through the overgrown garden, waist-high in weeds and wild roses, entering the ground floor through a french window consisting only of a rotting wooden frame.

A candle stood in a broken saucer on a shelf. They lighted

this and started to walk from room to room – cobwebs hung from the ceilings and the house was damp, smelling of the rotting floorboards which gave under their feet. Each room was more dank and depressing than the last.

Plaster had dropped from the ceilings in lumps, thick wallpaper hung in strips. The trio were so affected by the atmosphere and an inexplicable aura of evil that they started to drop their voices to a whisper as if they feared disturbing something.

A staircase stretched upwards into the darkness. Nichols had gone ahead and stood waiting for the others to join him. As he did so a curious feeling came over him. He had thought it would simply be creepy as any deserted house might be, but this was something else. The atmosphere had changed as if everything had gone into slow motion, even his sight was blurred as though some dark material had come between him and the outside world. He thought he was going to faint, but feared that if he did some terrible fate would overcome him.

He staggered down the stairs past the other two and outside, sinking thankfully on the damp soft grass and trembling from his experience. A stiff breeze had come up, the evening had turned cool, a window was flapping somewhere on rusted hinges. Getting shakily to his feet, he said he did not want to do any more exploring and suggested to the other two that they went on to meet their friends, but now there was no stopping them.

St Audries ran up the stairs and across the landing to the room where Nichols had been. The other two standing in the garden called after him to keep whistling and they would answer.

Abruptly, St Audries' answering whistle stopped as though someone had put a hand over his mouth.

There was utter silence. Even the breeze had dropped – no sound came from anywhere as if the world itself stood still, holding its breath.

Then a scream came from up the stairs – almost inhuman and yet they could recognise it as St Audries' voice. In his book Nichols said it was a sound 'which I hope I shall never hear again, the kind of cry a man who had been stabbed in the back would make.'

Now came the sound of a terrible struggle, thuds, screams. They ran into the house but St Audries almost knocked them flying in his headlong dash past them, his face ashen, his hair and clothes covered in dust.

At last he managed to speak through tight lips. 'The thing . . . it happened, out of the room and down the darkness of the corridor, something raced . . . it was black, shaped like a man. . .' He paused to gain his breath, leaning on a broken garden seat. 'I just noticed two things – the first was I could see no face, only blackness – the second was it made no noise as it raced at me over the rotting boards . . . no sound . . . knocking me flat. I had this terrible sensation of evil as though I was struggling with something completely inhuman, something dark, evil.'

When St Audries became more coherent, Nichols discovered it was the same room in which he had felt faint. Probably if he had stayed he would have suffered the same fate.

The three young men were by now thoroughly frightened and out of their depth. They went next door and explained the situation, saying one of them had felt ill. They were given brandy by the householder and its warmth gradually restored them to some kind of normality. From him they learnt the terrible significance of that little room at the top of the stairs. . .

Like the Elephant's Child in Kipling's *Just So Stories*, I have an insatiable curiosity and having read Nichols' account of this affair in his book *Twenty-Five* I had to see where Castel-a-Mare had once stood.

In the exact location described by Nichols, opposite a house called Edwinstowe there was a gaping hole like a missing tooth. A high stone wall ran along the road with a white gate in the middle which obviously had once led into the back premises and garden of a house. Next door on one side stood Norfolk Lodge and Grendon, on the other Monte Rosa. There was a big empty patch where once a three storey house had stood.

It was 1979 when I first saw the place. A Mr Reburn was living in Monte Rosa and I called to ask if he could tell me the story of Castel-a-Mare. However, it seems he had not lived there long and had not heard the tale from years ago, but he took me down some cement steps to his garden. This was well below the level of the road as it would have been the cellars of the house.

'I have often wondered why there is only about a foot of earth in my garden and beneath it stones and bricks,

Monte Rosa and the old stables, next to where Castel-a-Mare had stood.

obviously from the demolished house, as though a load of earth had been brought to cover them,' he told me. I wondered what else they might cover. He said that he had thought that from various tiles and things he had found on his premises that they had once been stables.

'As a matter of fact,' he went on, 'I did wonder from the number of names on the deeds that the house must have changed hands over and over again, but that is really all I know of the history of the place.'

And so I started to research this 'something out of hell', for I must admit that standing among the ruins somehow even the name – 'Castel-a-Mare' – seemed to hold a kind of intangible menace.

To begin at the beginning – it was very difficult from the small amount of information I could glean to decide who actually was the victim and who the assassin in what had obviously been a terrible murder or murders. In one account I read, the house had been owned by a local doctor who had periods of insanity and had murdered his wife and then the little maid who had witnessed the crime, while others said the victim was a guest who had come as a patient to stay with the doctor and whom he murdered. But perhaps after so many years it is not all that important who the victim was or his or her killer – more important is what they left behind.

For years the old house in the Warberries was haunted by the maid who witnessed the brutal murder. This story at least is universal and widespread. She screamed when she saw what was happening, then turned and ran, to be chased from room to room up and down the stairs and along the dark corridors until at last the murderer caught her and strangled her too, the body being put in a cupboard which was later incorporated into a bathroom. This was probably where Nichols and St Audries had their terrible experiences.

And so the ghost of Castel-a-Mare started to haunt the house and, it seems, the stables too, which were so affected that horses could only be forced into them backwards. No doors stayed locked, dogs would not pass the house without whimpering and howling, some owners even had actually to cross the road with them. No tenant would stay, as Mr Reburn had discovered, and eventually the house had fallen into such decay that lead was stolen from the roof, and timber and even bricks were taken. The tales of horror and mystery increased, as did the vandalism.

My fascination with the story increased. I went to talk to a lady by the name of Edna White who was a member of the Devonshire Association and lived in Torquay. She had collected mystery stories of Devon for 20 years and showed me some of the notes she had made from a book written by Violet Tweedale, *Ghosts I Have Seen*.

Violet herself lived in the Warberries and often passed the house. She had heard running footsteps and screams, and listened to gossip about the house and its inmates. Eventually she found out the man who owned it – a builder – and asked if she might make some investigations. He gave his consent.

This was the story Edna told me. The house was demolished in 1920 as a result of all the damage, but before that happened, in 1913 Violet and her husband made the first investigation. It produced very little except a feeling of intense cold and a chilling sensation as if they were being watched, she remarked, 'by something intensely evil.'

In 1917 Violet was asked to join a party of people who intended to investigate the house with the aid of a medium. This had come about through a soldier who was home on leave and was interested and very knowledgeable in psychic research – he had organised the party and invited several people including Violet.

The medium chose a bedroom on the first floor next to the bathroom. After some little time she suddenly started to give vent to a volley of violent language in the deep-toned voice of a man, asking what right all these intruders had to be in his house. There was a rather unpleasant scene, for although the medium was a comparatively elderly lady – and frail – suddenly she was controlled by this 'man' of superhuman strength who bellowed out terrible language, without warning attacking the soldier and throwing him to the ground. Two others in the party had to go to his aid, but with herculean strength the medium threw them all back against the wall, forcing them to the top of the stairs, obviously with the intention of throwing them down. There was a scuffle during which the onlookers were helpless. Any moment it seemed someone would be seriously injured.

Then as suddenly as the poor woman had been possessed, it all ended. The medium crashed to the floor, the onlookers fearing she must be dead. Quickly they picked her up and took her out into the fresh air where gradually she recovered. Someone had a brandy flask and this revived her. And then to everyone's amazement, the soldier asked her if she felt inclined to repeat the experiment a few days later.

The others protested that it would be cruel, asking for trouble, but she agreed. It might risk her life, they said, but she was adamant.

So a week later they all gathered once more in the house. One or two other people had heard of the last event and joined the original party. This time the soldier assured them he was prepared – he did seem to have considerable experience in this kind of happening and stated he intended to exorcise the 'entity' as he described it – whoever or whatever 'it' might be.

This led to an almost incredible encounter in which, as in a boxing ring, the fight swayed back and forth between one protagonist and another.

At first it seemed the soldier would overcome the medium and she started to cry as if she had changed into a heartbroken young girl. She babbled incoherently between sobs that shook her – 'Poor master . . . there on the bed . . . help him, help him. . .' over and over again – then clenched her hands to her throat as if she were trying to tear away other hands that were strangling her. Was this the culmination of some horrifying murder that had occurred on that very spot?

Suddenly the air was rent by the most piercing, bloodcurdling screams as the medium now turned as if she were an animal at bay, struggling with something unseen, wrestling wildly, fighting for her very own life while all the time the terrible screams came from her.

In vain the others tried to help her, to drag her away from this invisible murderer, but it was impossible to seize an intangible, disembodied spirit.

At last two of the onlookers managed to get her against the wall and stood in front so they could try to defend her against the original spirit which had controlled her. The poor woman was gasping for breath, trying to speak in a young girl's voice, hoarse with emotion.

'He'll kill me next! He's killed the master! Someone help!'

At last the power of the soldier's exorcism apparently triumphed – if that was indeed what it was. He managed to control the medium and discover from the spirit that possessed her that the man had been insane when the murder took place and she was the little maid who shared the victim's fate – but whether the victim was the doctor or the patient did not become clear.

Violet Tweedale tracked down the records which verified the names and dates of the various residents of the villa but by then, of course, these violent events had all taken place at least 50 years before and there was no one alive who could confirm the actual story.

If it is true, and I have no reason to doubt it, it does have to fall into the category of the perfect murder, for no record of any killing is recorded in those times by anyone who was then alive.

In her book Mrs Tweedale added something which interested me very much and was to come to mind years later. She said, 'I do not know if it is intended to build another house on the same site, I hope not for it is very probable even a new residence would share the fate of the old – bricks and mortar are no impediment to the disembodied and there is no reason why they should not elect to manifest within an indefinite period of time.'

Her account is dated 1920 which would make the date of the murder sometime in about 1870.

Edna White told me she had tried to trace the owners and tenants of the property but up to now all she had found was a Mrs Dove in 1857 and a Mr Benjamin Fulwood in 1878/9. It was owned by a builder whose name she thought was E. P. Bovey and he lived opposite in Edwinstowe.

When I asked her what she thought of the whole affair she added one explanation for there being no recording of the murder: if it was the patient who died, the male victim, said to be a foreigner, could have been given a death certificate by the doctor who murdered him and thus a normal burial. But what about the little maid, what happened to her body?

A couple of summers ago I went back to see what had happened, if anything, to the shades of Castel-a-Mare. A huge new house was being built. I talked to the builders who were having a tea break.

'Anything odd happened here at all?' I asked. For a moment they just grinned at me, 'another barmy old bird' I expect they thought. Then one put down his mug.

'Well, we did think some vandals had been in and moved our ladders and upset tins of paint. We'd locked them all up and no one had actually broken in – it's the new bathroom top of the stairs – made us feel a bit spooky.'

The garden wall, showing the white gate still in situ while the new building rises behind.

I decided not to tell them about the 'something out of hell'. They might be tempted to pass it on to the new owner and as my old Devonshire granny used to say, 'What you don't know can't hurt you.'

Not too sure in this case.

The Wrecker
William Oatway

SMUGGLING as a trade or profession is not exactly one that can advertise its success. If those who practise it wish to stay out of jail, they keep their mouths shut. But fortunately some of the tales of these men from the past who also practised wrecking, have come down to us.

Wrecking involved the use of lamps shone from the cliffs and shore to lure ships off course to small bays, estuaries or inlets where they were wrecked on unmarked, submerged rocks, enabling them to be robbed of their cargoes. Quite often murder was involved along with the robbery of jewels and money from passengers as well as crew, and it was in this 'trade' that William Oatway of Chambercombe Manor in North Devon excelled.

The Manor dates back to the 12th century and lies about a mile inland from Ilfracombe. It is reputed to have a tunnel reaching from the house to Hele Bay, lending itself to smuggling. Ilfracombe itself was noted for this illegal trade as many big ships came in there during its heyday. In fact the Collector at the time, that is the official who collected taxes and imposed fines on smugglers when they were caught, swore that most of the pilot boats were engaged in the illegal and extremely profitable practice.

The house itself is haunted beyond doubt, too many rational people have confirmed this for it to be discounted,

Chambercombe Manor, which dates back to the 12th century.

but it is not quite clear by whom the manifestation is made. In fact there are differing opinions in the matter. Some say it is the ghost of Kate Oatway, daughter of William. Others that it is the shade of Lady Jane Grey who, in the mid 1500s shortly before she was executed, was said to have slept there.

Strange as it may seem, the Window Tax of 1696 plays an important role in this haunting. When it was first brought in as law those having to pay it were little different from the taxpayers of today and sought to avoid it in any manner possible, using such methods as blocking up with bricks any windows which were not essential to daily living. If you look at old buildings you may still see traces of these in situ.

In 1865 the tenant of the Manor was a farmer named John Vyles. Whether window cleaners existed in those days history does not relate, possibly a nagging wife had driven her husband to do the job, but in any case as he cleaned it was inevitable he should notice a bricked up portion of the wall where obviously there had once been a small window.

Even after 200 years perhaps it did not blend exactly with the older wall. However, from outside he realised there was not any room in the house to justify the window's past existence.

Hurrying indoors he visited each upstairs room and every window – he was right, there was an odd man out.

With great excitement – possibly at the thought of hidden treasure – Vyles got a pickaxe and breaking through the connecting wall of the other bedroom, found a small hidden room.

Gradually his eyes grew accustomed to the dim light and the dust and began to make out its sinister contents. Cobwebs hanging from the ceiling brushed his face as, candle in hand, he moved towards the centre of the room where a fourposter bed stood half concealed by rotting curtains. Round the wall hung the rich material of tapestries in torn fragments, while a chair and a dressing table with tarnished mirror stood against one wall.

The sweat broke out on his forehead and body as he gazed at the skeleton on the bed. It proved to be of a young woman, a few rags of female clothing still covering the white bones.

As there was no identification for the body – or rather, skeleton for that is all there was – Vyles had it buried in a pauper's grave in Ilfracombe churchyard. I find it odd that no enquiries were made at this juncture.

So the rumours started – the first that it was Kate Oatway, daughter of William who had lived at the Manor in the 17th century.

The generally accepted version of this story is that she found out what her father was up to and threatened to expose him to the authorities as a noted wrecker. Kate had probably come by boat from Ireland to visit her parents in Ilfracombe for she was married to Tristan Wallace, an officer in the Irish Army. By an odd quirk of fate, the very ship she was in had been drawn to the rocks by her own father with his gang of wreckers. It was often the custom of these men – apart from robbery – to kill any passengers on board to make sure their mouths were kept shut; they even murdered the crews. One story is that Oatway killed her at the scene of the wreck and then possibly her body had been carried through the tunnel to the small room. If she had not already been killed then this room was to be her living tomb, bricked up until she starved to death, and people said her ghost haunted the house trying to take revenge on her father.

Yet another alternative is that it was not Kate, but the skeleton of some titled lady who had also come to North Devon to visit relatives and whose body had been hidden after she had been robbed and murdered.

The North Devon author, Daniel Farson's fascinating book on ghosts brings in another suspect in the shape of William Oatway's father, Alexander. According to this version, he was the wrecker (keeping the business in the family!) and it was the son who found the body of the woman in the wrecked ship. Already dead, she had been so badly battered she was unrecognisable. He could not resist the temptation of robbery. However, later when the admiralty authorities enquired about a missing person William bluffed his way out only to discover to his horror the person of whom they spoke was his own daughter. Farson goes on to say his confession was found years later behind a fireplace in a house in Fowey where he had died.

A very different tale is that the ghost is that of Lady Jane Grey, who was queen for only nine days before she was beheaded in 1554. Apart from the Champernowne family who had once, among many others, owned the Manor, it had also been part of the estate of Lord Grey in Devon so perhaps Jane too had been visiting relatives in the area – although she certainly had not been killed there!

Whatever version is correct matters little as one thing is

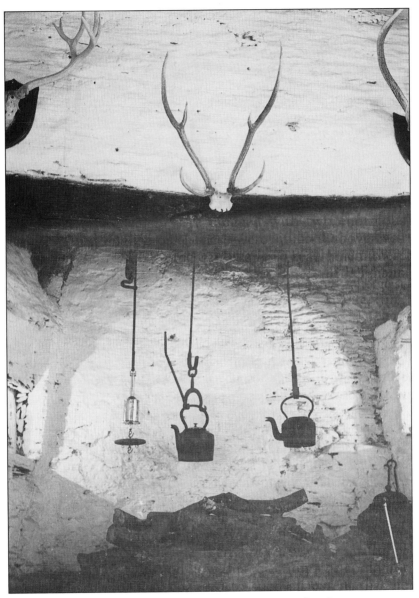

The kitchen at Chambercombe Manor, with its vast fireplace.

certain, something strange does go on at Chambercombe Manor which defies logical explanation. Footsteps are heard climbing a staircase which no longer is there; the steps on the stairs are laboured as though they are of someone carrying a heavy load such as a corpse. A girl in great distress has been seen in the corridors, passing in and out of the Lady Jane Bedroom, through what was once the Great Hall and along the passage to the chapel. Odd sounds of someone in distress come from the closed, empty room between the two bedrooms.

Many of the tour guides to the house have had odd experiences. One was in charge of a party when a young lady dressed in what were described as pale clothes asked if she could follow the party round, which she did. When the visit ended in the courtyard there was no sign of her. She had spoken to no one else.

Many and varied people have definitely spoken of experiencing an aura or presence. I found it very atmospheric too, thinking about that young girl, whoever she was, who had experienced a terrible storm, to be thrown wet and shivering on the beach where she was robbed and either murdered or dragged up the tunnel to the room where she was to suffer slow death from starvation, where no one would hear her faint cries for help.

No wonder her spirit remains to remind us of either her violent – or worse, her long drawn out – death.

'SEA BED HUNT FOR LOST WIFE'

IN the *Mail On Sunday* dated 9th July 2000 the headline read: 'MISTRESS IN VANISHED WIFE MURDER HUNT RETURNS TO CONFRONT HER EX-LOVER'S PAST.'

For a moment I was about to turn the page – just another 'domestic'; the police always say there are more of these assaults than any other kind.

Then I saw the photograph and recognised the face of Eunice Chapman whom I not only had known in the past but interviewed in the early 1980s when she had left Salcombe to live in a tiny village in the South Hams.

Eunice was – and still is – a beautiful woman, sophisticated and efficient as she always was in her day as the chief restauranteur in Salcombe. During the interview in the 1980s we discovered we were also fellow writers as her book *Presumed Dead*, her autobiography as Eunice Yabsley, had been published.

She talked freely to me about her life with John Allen and the extraordinary story of his wife Pat and their two children who had mysteriously disappeared in 1975 and of whom no trace has ever been found.

I first remember Eunice when we lived in the South Hams. She was a widow struggling to bring up three children and run her restaurant – The Galley, in Salcombe. We called in there for a meal whenever we visited the town for her food

Lifeboat Quay, Salcombe.

was first class and she always looked smart and beautifully
groomed even if she had been toiling over a hot stove,
pleased to greet people whether local or on holiday, liked by
everyone.

She and her husband Charlie Yabsley had built up a
successful business over 14 years. Charlie himself had been
one of the best known and most charismatic characters in
Salcombe and when he died Eunice had succeeded him as
Chairman of the old Salcombe District Council, for he was
much admired and involved in public life.

Early in 1975 a family moved into the town who were not
only to change Eunice's life but would also thrust Salcombe
from its peaceful serenity into the uneasy light of the
national press. Gossip, malice and suspicion would surface

as it turned over the layers of human relationships and opened a proverbial can of worms.

John and Pat Allen with their two children, Jonathan aged seven and six year old Victoria, had been living in a caravan in Dawlish. They had had a fairly unsettled marriage, both emotionally and physically in that they had moved from town to town, city to city. John was not very successful at holding down a job – perhaps a little inclined to be unreliable as we shall see later. Anyway, Pat had met him in 1967. His name actually was Anthony John Allen but he had also been known as Anthony John Angel. They had married at Halifax Register Office on 8th March 1968. Jonathan was born in the following January and they then moved to High Lane, Cheshire where Victoria was born in May 1970. They moved to Kettering and in 1971 were living in Leicester. Between March 1971 and April 1972 John was self employed, working away from home, but eventually he went bankrupt. What his work was is not clear, but it meant Pat was left on her own.

She was an excellent mother but at her age was used to a fairly good social life and very much enjoyed the company of men, a volatile personality who needed something beyond children and housework – there is no harm in that. During John's absence she had many men friends. However, any differences there may have been between husband and wife were settled and in 1974 they decided to make a completely fresh start and move south.

This took them to a caravan site in Dawlish, South Devon. Pat got a good job as a receptionist, she was a beautician and with her looks and personality she would have been a great asset to any business.

While they were there John found a job at the New Grand Hotel in Torquay, from whence he went on to work as restaurant manager at the very prestigious Marine Hotel in Salcombe for £50 a week, a good wage in those days. He would have been kept very busy as the hotel attracted visitors from the Midlands, London and all over England for the yachting in the area and the luxury the hotel offered. It had belonged to the Ryder family for many years as did the famous Ferry Inn, a well known venue for show biz personnel, especially during the war.

John had excellent references from the Torquay hotel and best of all a flat went with the job in a beautiful house – Powderham Villa in Devon Road in Salcombe.

Pat was over the moon. She was a real homemaker and had had plenty of experience in her married life of moving around, so she set about completely altering the kitchen, painting and decorating, making curtains – probably standing at the window and gazing out over the estuary

Pat Allen loved her home in Powderham Villa, with its views over the estuary.

while she took the necessary measurements. The view was fabulous with the constantly moving traffic of boats, from luxurious yachts to the fishing boats and dinghies.

She was gregarious by nature and soon made friends with her neighbours in the flat below, Brenda and Mike Jones. He was a hotel chef and it was to Brenda Pat had said, 'This is the perfect place for the kids to grow up in – just what I have always wanted.'

It was during these few months that John got to know Eunice. He probably noticed The Galley and saw the beautiful woman who ran her business so efficiently; naturally he would drop in for a drink. This became quite a regular occurrence, they were both crossword fanatics and sat at the bar solving these together.

Most of the girls in Salcombe remember John as a great charmer. Broad shouldered, tall, he strode around the port with a distinctive walk which you could recognise even from a distance. It is no wonder that Eunice, a lonely widow with three children, her own father also having just died, trying to run a business on her own, should turn to this man for solace.

For a little while all went well with the Allens – then John told Eunice he thought Pat was having an affair with someone else. By now she was in love with him herself but had no intention of taking him from his wife – it was just an affair, but he was kind, gentle and affectionate, assuring her his marriage was virtually over and that Pat had threatened to leave him.

May Bank Holiday was the day of Marlborough Carnival, the neighbouring village to Salcombe. This particular year was to stand out in the memory of all the people in the area for it was the last known public sighting of Pat and her two children.

The morning after the carnival Brenda had gone up to the Allens' flat to have a good gossip with Pat. There would have been much to talk about, having met so many friends at that happy affair. To her surprise she found John on his own.

'Pat has gone away for a few days,' he told her. 'It's a bit awkward with the children.'

'I'll willingly take them, I'm very fond of them,' Brenda said.

Quickly John shook his head. 'Thanks very much, but there's no need, my mother is coming from Bournemouth to look after them.'

Rather curiously, it came out later that John had asked Eunice if she would take the children, in spite of the fact he had refused Brenda's offer. However, Eunice said it was quite impossible with her own three and the business to look after, the busy season just starting.

He told Eunice he and Pat had had a flaming row during the afternoon of the carnival, and that when he got back to the flat from work that evening she was packing her belongings preparatory to leaving.

'She drove off in the Volkswagen leaving the two children behind, she said she was going out of my life forever. I gave her £70 to help her on her way.'

It seems in the event she must have come back and collected the children two days later, as they too disappeared. In any case, as a result of all this upset he lost his job at the Marine Hotel. That meant he also had no home.

Immediately, warm-hearted Eunice offered him a job and home in The Galley. Gossip, which had been fermenting under the surface of the town, now burst out in an explosion of hate and malice.

Three months passed and then one of Pat's cousins from Halifax arrived in Salcombe to see why she had not written her regular letter for such a long time. It was then Pat's car, the Volkswagen, was found on Shadycombe Car Park where it had stood for all that time. No one had taken any particular notice or remarked on it. As a result the police at once started their investigation, cross questioning John, expressing their surprise that Pat had made so few preparations if she had intended to disappear. There was money owing to her from the beauty parlour where she worked, she had left new clothes she had just bought, the children's favourite toys. But John had an answer for all this.

'She obviously meant to make a clean break – I thought she'd gone off with one of her many boyfriends, even perhaps to America. In fact she went so far as to say she was only taking things which I had NOT given her.' It was proved she could not have left the country as she had no passport. The police were highly suspicious that he had not reported her disappearance long ago.

Brenda and Mike were questioned, specially about John's 17 foot cabin cruiser and the small dinghy which had disappeared on the same day as Pat. It was generally used for ferrying the friends back and forth to parties on the boat, or fishing trips.

The press too were not giving up. This was when the *Daily Mail* headline 'SEA BED HUNT FOR LOST WIFE' appeared in June 1976. The disappearance of the dinghy pointed to the bodies having been dropped in the sea. The general opinion of the CID was that Pat had been murdered and the murderer then returned to kill the children who could have witnessed the whole affair. But there was no shred of evidence. Divers searched the whole area for what by this time would be twelve-month old skeletons – hardly more, taking into consideration the grim reality of crabs in the area.

The reason this scandal so shocked and scandalised the people of Salcombe was that it involved Eunice, one of their own. John was still living at The Galley. Repeatedly he told the police, 'I would never have harmed my wife or children, I had no motive, a good job, a lovely home. Why would I want to destroy all that?'

Pat Allen's disappearance, and those of her children, has never been solved.

However, in her latest interview Eunice says she now realises, a generation on, that he was a schemer and wanted to secure his future. 'It was so overwhelming at the time, I just could not sort out the strands. . .'

In 1982 the lease on The Galley ran out and the couple split up. Allen opened another restaurant in London – by now he was carrying on 'his usual philandering with other women. Eunice added, 'Things were never the same again after Salcombe – John took up with several others, we went our separate ways.' Eunice trained for a job as sub editor on nursing magazines.

It was when I heard she had left Salcombe that I went to talk to her, and later to Chief Detective Superintendent John Bisset at the HQ of the Devon Police at Middlemoor in Exeter.

'The file is still open', he told me, 'for months we welcomed information and clues. We used to have people coming forward with hunches every week. Eventually interest dwindled, people forgot.'

It seems in the anxiety to clear himself John Allen had written to the American Embassy asking if they could put him in touch with any newspaper or organisation that could help. He even asked a friend who was visiting the USA to ask the Salvation Army if there was anything they could suggest. But nothing came of any enquiries.

Chief Detective Superintendent Bisset told me, 'In my opinion everything points to the sad fact that mother and children are dead, we have no evidence otherwise – but that is only my opinion. Perhaps there is a rational explanation, Pat may be living a normal life somewhere. If so, even after all this time we appeal to her to contact the police, our only concern is for their welfare – of the mother and children. We have no wish to become involved in any way in a domestic affair, but the Force will not rest until the mystery is solved.'

For many years Eunice refused to countenance the gossip

over Pat's disappearance and in fact when I talked to her all those years ago she still firmly believed Allen was innocent, but as the police delved even more deeply into the case she did admit that he told too many lies, layer upon layer until it was difficult to find where the truth lay.

The material the press dug out about the Allens once they took an interest makes fascinating reading. Pat had been born Patricia Jean Blackler in Keighley, Yorkshire, in 1935. She married Marcus Walker in 1956 and separated the following year. She then became very friendly with an American Air Force officer and spent several months in the USA and Canada. In 1967 she came back to England and met John 'Angel' as he called himself then. He had been a con man, bankrupt and fraudster; when he met Pat he was already a bigamist. During his first marriage he had faked suicide by swimming out to sea and leaving a pile of clothes and a suicide note – quite a fashion at one time. His bigamy was discovered when an old friend bumped into him and said he thought 'Angel' was dead. He managed to escape jail because Pat stood by him. It seems John had started life with every opportunity – a grammar school education, prospective employment as an architect. He had joined the Royal Engineers at the age of 18 and reached the rank of Sergeant in 1968, leaving with an exemplary record.

Today Pat would be in her seventies, the children in their thirties – if they are still alive. One theory, a purely personal one, is that she went back to her past love in the USA taking the children with her. She had ample time to get out of the country before any enquiries were made, on a forged passport or that of an American perhaps – and why should she later want to disclose her whereabouts? I do not feel she owed John anything in particular but although he may have been every kind of rogue and cad – oddly, so attractive a type to many women – this does not necessarily mean he would commit murder.

This does not make the affair any less extraordinary. As

the police maintain, as far as they can see no crime was committed with which anyone can be charged, in fact these people might never have existed except for Eunice who talked to me so freely in the past – a woman who once lived with a man who could have been a murderer. Does someone out there know the answers?

In the recent interview reported in the *Mail on Sunday* Eunice said, 'I'd do anything I could to help discover what really happened – I suppose I should hate John but I find it easier to be indifferent.'

What is a happy ending to all this is that Eunice, back in her home town of Salcombe, is accepted – greeted with

OUTCAST'S RETURN: Eunice in Salcombe where she was vilified

Eunice Chapman has now returned to Salcombe. (By kind permission of the Mail on Sunday)

smiles as her neighbours meet her in the street, the past forgotten. She is still 'one of ours'.

And meanwhile the search for answers to Pat Allen's disappearance goes on. In July this year, the police confirmed that they are bringing the investigation up to date and the case once more made the headlines in the *Western Morning News*. As Chief Detective Superintendent John Bissett told me all those years ago – 'the Force will not rest until the mystery is solved'.

THE MAGIC ISLAND

LUNDY lies in the Bristol Channel a little more than eleven miles off the North Devon coast – dramatic, windswept and breathtakingly beautiful. Like all islands it beckons with a kind of magic; often wreathed in mist it has an aura of intrigue and yet a deep peace.

Technically it is a lump of granite of about 1,100 acres, three miles long and half a mile wide, wild land exposed to the elements. Belonging to Devon, it is part of the hundred of Braunton.

But what a history it has had for such a small area. When I went there as a small child, a wonderful man called Felix Gade was resident agent for the Harman family who owned it. He and his wife lived on the island until his death in the 1970s. He acted as postmaster for all mail both inwards and outwards. There was nothing about Lundy and its history that he did not know. While my uncles and aunt wandered among the pink thrift, sat at their easels sketching or stood on the highest point – Beacon Hill – looking at the magnificent views, Wales in one direction and the Devon and Cornish coast in the other, Felix told me the wonderful, thrilling, romantic stories of the island's past. He taught me to call it Lundy, not Lundy Island, as the name comes from the old Norse words 'lundi' meaning puffin and 'ey' meaning island so you have Lundy – Puffin Island. The island is still renowned for its puffins and these intriguing little birds are its logo.

He and his wife were the only residents on the island during the Second World War, apart from six lighthouse keepers, facing the not unlikely occurrence of landing and occupation by the enemy. More of this later . . .

As a child what I felt most was the boundless space and freedom. Watching at night from the window in the guest house I could see the lights of the ships moving about their business up and down the Bristol Channel. In spite of its position open to the four winds of heaven, the island is a mass of colour at all times of the year with wild flowers, rhododendrons, purple ling – every hue from blue to yellow.

From time immemorial the island has been inhabited, used as a refuge by pirates and smugglers, a place for infamous goings on and said to be haunted. The Vikings used it as a base for raids on the mainland, the Normans took it over in the 12th century and it is their name – Marisco – which is found on the island today. It has had many owners – in 1834 William Hudson Heaven bought it and it became known as the Kingdom of Heaven; he built a

Lundy – 'dramatic, windswept and breathtakingly beautiful'. (By kind permission of the Landmark Trust)

mansion which he named Millcombe. At the end of the First World War it was sold to Augustus Langham Christie, and in 1925 he sold it to Martin Coles Harman. When Albion Harman died in 1968 the island was put up for sale. There were fears of developers ruining its unique beauty but the Landmark Trust underwrote a worldwide appeal to raise the money to buy the island. It was then the millionaire, Jack Hayward made a gift of £150,000 towards the purchase, and the National Trust was able to go ahead, buying the island and leasing it to the Landmark Trust who had the mammoth task of carefully restoring the buildings and services, generally tidying up for visitors and residents alike.

What of the former occupants of the island? It was literally a nest and lair of pirates and smugglers in the 16th century, and woe betide anyone who was unlucky enough to become wrecked on its vicious coast. In the 1700s Captain Kidd was notorious as the chief of the pirates, worshipped by young boys much as pop starts are today, but even he was caught at last.

Today there is still talk of buried treasure, as the infamous Captain Nutt is said to have left gold worth a king's ransom in a cave at the foot of a 365 foot cliff. He had been forced to flee from Lundy after, returning one day from a raid, his ship was intercepted by two British men-o'war. In 1864 two men went in search of this gold but they became trapped by the tide and a fall of rock; it was 70 years before their bodies were found. This brought about the belief that there is a curse on the treasure and that the cave is haunted by the ghosts of the two men and perhaps Nutt himself, and they will bring death to anyone who attempts to remove the gold.

Thomas Benson was perhaps even more famous a character. He had a contract with the government to transport convicts to Maryland and Virginia, and he certainly left his stamp on the island. He was a merchant in Bideford, High Sheriff of Devon and MP for Barnstaple in

1747. As lessee of Lundy and transporter of convicts, he was careful none of these poor creatures ever reached America. He put them to work in the quarry, farming, and building walls. He fired a gun at any passing ships which looked as though they might come to investigate. He also was deeply involved in smuggling and even has a cave named after him. Eventually he was found out; he fled to Portugal where he died in 1772.

There was a time when quarrying the granite brought rich rewards. Horses pulled tubs of stone along a tramway, and then the blocks were taken by boat from Quarry beach which must have been a mammoth task in itself. All of this was built by Benson's convicts. At one time there was even a Lundy Granite Company but that was in 1868 and it only lasted five years before it was wound up with the company in financial difficulties. Obviously honesty did not pay as well as piracy, although Lundy granite was used in the building of the Thames embankment, several Devon churches and a famous London hotel.

Another mystery is connected with Lance Corporal John Pennington Harman, the eldest son of Martin Harman, the owner of the island at the time. John was killed in Burma during the Second World War, and was posthumously awarded the Victoria Cross. He was a keen naturalist and beekeeper, and five thousand miles away on Lundy his hive of bees all died at the same time as their owner. There is an old tale in Devon that when the owner of a hive of bees dies they must be told at once so they can mourn or else they too will die. Either someone did not know of this or forgot to tell them.

The wrecks around Lundy are too numerous to recount. Many are not even recorded, the sheer cliffs and jagged rocks making rescue almost impossible in some cases. The one which perhaps caused the most publicity was that of the battleship *Montague* in 1906. In 1901 when she was launched she had cost a million pounds, a giant of her time

The sheer cliffs and treacherous rocks that have brought so many ships to their doom. (By kind permission of the Landmark Trust)

with a crew of 750. She was serving with the Channel Fleet, testing new radio equipment, when she ran aground on the rocks in thick fog due to a miscalculation by the navigating officer who thought he was off Hartland Point. No lives were lost but although the Admirality sent a small fleet of sister ships, a cruiser and tugs to try and rescue the ship, she could not be saved.

Lundy still claims its victims in spite of all modern technology. During the Second World War a drama of another kind occurred when in March 1941 a Heinkel bomber, which had been involved in a major raid on Swansea, had to make a forced landing on Lundy. The crew were unhurt and immediately set fire to their plane. The men surrendered to Felix Gade without a fight and were shipped to the mainland.

Strangely enough, only a few weeks later another Heinkel on the same mission over Swansea flew into the cliffs, killing the crew. The plane this time disintegrated. In June 1942 an English Whitley bomber did exactly the same thing, killing its crew of seven.

Of course, many ships were added to the wrecks during that war as a result of enemy action. Some were driven ashore, while others tried to make land after being torpedoed or hitting mines, most eventually being destroyed by the ever pounding seas.

A lighthouse was erected in 1819, but fog frequently obscured this, so in 1897 the North Light and South Light at either end of the island were built as substitutes.

Today the trip to Lundy is a great deal simpler than when I visited. The MS *Oldenburg* runs from Bideford or Ilfracombe all the year round, for anyone interested in wildlife, rock climbing, birdwatching or just relaxing away from traffic and hustle. Lundy exists in what appears to be a time warp, with the benefits of modern life, but an atmosphere of the mysterious past.

THE CORPSE ON THE MOOR

RESEARCHING is one of a writer's most fascinating jobs because whilst doing so for one subject, inevitably something else immediately seizes your interest and leads you down a primrose path far removed from your original plan.

This happened many times when I was writing about Beatrice Chase, that wonderful writer who was the first one to bring Dartmoor alive for so many people – called by John Oxenham 'My Lady of the Moor'.

Among some papers in the library I found a small paperback entitled *The Corpse on the Moor*, written by Beatrice when she was living at Widecombe-in-the-Moor, the heart of her beloved Devon.

What a title! It was published in 1946 and on the flyleaf was an extract from the *Western Morning News* of 15th August in that year which reads as follows: 'Miss Beatrice Chase, well known authoress who lives at Widecombe-in-the-Moor, has written a mystery story *The Corpse on the Moor* based on the facts concerning the discovery of a body on Dartmoor on November 6th 1934. The mystery, which was never solved, aroused considerable interest throughout the country. The body was identified as that of Walton Howard, a native of Warrington, but the cause of death was never established. Miss Chase befriended the mother of Mr

Howard. She played an active part in attempts to throw light on the case'.

Beatrice added, 'In the story I am about to tell everyone is now dead and as the crime, if crime it was, is still unsolved, the full truth can hurt no one'.

On the morning of 6th November 1934, the *Western Morning News* contained an account of the finding of the body of an unknown man at Postbridge, the central village of Dartmoor with the first clapper bridge over the Dart from the river's rise at Cranmere Pool.

The body had been found on land known as Archerton Newtake a mile from Postbridge post office. The funeral, in a nameless coffin, was to take place that day. The coffin had no name plate or description, a situation which was believed to be unique in the district.

There were several emblems of sympathy, including a

The clapper bridge at Postbridge, near where the body was found.

The grave of the unknown man.

wreath of Flanders poppies tied up with black ribbon from Sir Courtenay Bennett of Archerton near where the body was found. There was also a bunch of chrysanthemums with no inscription, and another of the same flowers tied with blue from Beatrice Chase herself. The card attached read 'With the deepest sympathy to an unknown fellow creature from My Lady of the Moor on behalf of his unknown mother'.

The body had been found by John Bailey, a farmer from Merripit, a moorlander who had lived all his life in central Dartmoor. It was lying at the head of a stream in a clump of bushes. Beside it were a collar, a tie, a tanners' knife, a candle, an empty brown bottle without a cork, and the dead man's left shoe was lying on the ground beside him. In his pockets were a manicure set, some very small change, and a watch which had the large hand removed. Later in this story the mystery deepens concerning the watch hand and the left shoe.

There was no apparent cause of death. The body was badly decomposed and of course forensic science was not as advanced as it is today.

On 10th November a short account appeared in the press saying it had been discovered that the man was a native of Warrington in Lancashire. His name was Walton Howard. Beatrice immediately wrote to the chief constable enclosing a letter of sympathy to the mother of the man.

Mrs Howard replied saying he was a much beloved only child. They had been appalled to learn of his terrible fate on Dartmoor. People in his home town had known him all his life, many had been to school with him. For the past five years he had been working in Bolton, going home at week ends. It was from that town he disappeared on 25th August.

No reason for that disappearance could be found. Adverts in the papers, police notices, letters and queries were all to no avail. Mrs Howard said how touched and grateful she was to the moorland people in attending his burial. She finished her letter, 'We are coming to Devonshire to attend the adjourned inquest. We hope to make arrangements to bring our dear son home.'

This information only intensified the mystery. How on earth had Walton ever reached a place so far away from Lancashire as Postbridge! Where was he from 25th August to 6th November, how and why had he come?

After much rearranging of both dates and venue, the adjourned inquest was fixed for 10th January at Postbridge.

Beatrice wrote many times to Mrs Howard, but still there was no ray of light on the whole affair. The first clue his mother had had of the affair was on 6th November when a friend in Warrington saw the account in the *Daily Mail* and took the paper to her in case it might be important.

When she read it she said, 'Postbridge? Where is Postbridge, where is Dartmoor? We know nothing and no one in such parts, it cannot be our Walton'.

On re-reading the account she discovered that the things found by the body sounded like her son's, yet how could he have got so far and to such an unknown place? But for the newspaper accounts probably Walton's identity would never have been discovered.

Now comes perhaps the most bizarre part in the whole story, for three weeks after the identity of Walton Howard was established, and before the inquest, a similar affair was reported from Sussex.

The body of an unknown man had been found at the foot of Beachy Head – a well known place for suicides on the Sussex coast. An account of this was published in the *Eastbourne Chronicle* on 1st December 1934.

The inquest was opened by the East Sussex Coroner, Dr E. F. Hoare at the Town Hall. This was adjourned for a fortnight as there was no evidence who the man was or how he came to fall over the cliff. A post mortem by Dr Geoffrey Shera said there was no indication of any internal disorder being the immediate cause of death; one lung was waterlogged. Death was due to the shock of so many injuries sustained by a fall and accelerated by being in the sea.

A Mr Arthur Ball of Dennis Road in Eastbourne said he was walking along the beach at 9.15 on Saturday morning and 500 yards west of the lighthouse saw a man lying face down on the beach. He was dead and had apparently fallen over the cliff. He appeared to be between 40 and 45 years, slightly bald with dark hair. He wore a brown suit and there was a trilby hat nearby. The body was just on the highwater mark. Mr Ball informed the police of his discovery.

Police Sergeant Arnold rowed to Beachy Head at 1 pm on Saturday and found the fully clothed body – nearby was a trilby hat and a shoe. The minute hand of the man's watch was missing, but the small hand indicated a time just before 5 o'clock so if he had fallen over the cliff at 5 pm on Friday the high tide would have reached him about midnight.

In the clothing was £1 10s in notes and 6s 6d in silver and copper. A silver cigarette case bore the initials GM, which initials were also on his socks. His broken silver watch had a silver chain and on the third finger of his left hand was a gold ring set with one diamond. There were no letters or documents of any kind on him.

Seeing this account, Beatrice at once got in touch with a reporter in Eastbourne and gave him an account of Walton Howard and the extraordinary coincidence between this and the corpse on the moor, with the removal in each case of the watch hand and the left shoe lying beside both of them.

He took it to the police. The identity of the man was soon discovered and confirmed by his brother Leslie Miller – he was George Miller aged 31, an unemployed ship's steward from Bolton, the same town from which Walton Howard had come. His brother had no idea why he was in Eastbourne or that there was any connection with Beachy Head, any more than Walton had with Dartmoor.

At the inquest held on 19th December 1934 it was said it was virtually impossible that there was not some connection between the two cases involving the removal of the watch hands and the shoes in the identical position. But a suicide does not remove the hand from his watch nor place a shoe beside himself.

Now the national press really went to town on the whole affair – or rather two affairs. The *Daily Telegraph* suggested that both men had become entangled in a Secret Society which they had at first believed to be an English Friendly Society. When they discovered it was a foreign set-up plotting against England they backed out and passed on their information. As a result the two apparently 'accidental' deaths were arranged in identical manner as an already agreed 'warning' to any other members of the Society who intended to act in a similar way. There was no solution in either case. The inquest on the Beachy Head victim was closed with a verdict of 'Found Dead'.

Now to return to the story of Walton. When he was last seen at noon on Saturday, 25th August, he left the tannery in Bolton where he worked as usual, dressed in a brown suit, carrying a suitcase and raincoat. This looked as if he intended to visit somewhere out of his usual routine, which was to return to Warrington from Saturday midday till Sunday evening.

When his body was found it was clothed in a grey suit – the brown suit, raincoat and suitcase were never found. He must have stayed somewhere to change into the grey, but where or when? Someone must have known. Lodgings in the area were all fine-combed, bus companies, railway booking offices – not a shred of information emerged.

Mrs Howard sent Beatrice a photo of Walton. It was a poor print but she took it to the police. The man who had first seeen the corpse said, 'This is not the man we found'. The police themselves had issued a circular giving a description of the missing man and bearing a photo of the corpse. Beatrice and the police compared the two photos; there was no resemblance between the two. Beatrice then asked Mrs Howard if the photo in the circular was a better likeness than the one she had sent. She replied that the one the police sent showed a spotted tie beside the body but it was a striped one that he always wore, one she had given him, he never wore spots as he hated them. She added that the photo for the police had been supplied by the friend with whom Walton lodged.

All this emphasised the fact that the decomposed body itself had not been identified, only the articles found beside him and the grey suit in which he was clothed – all those could have been stolen by someone else.

Finally at the inquest Mrs Howard said they had not seen him since the night of Sunday, 19th August when he left home to return to Bolton. 'He always left home in the same

Walton Howard.

way, we saw him to the door, he kissed me and said goodbye to his father who patted him on the shoulder and said, "Take care of yourself my boy and God bless you".'

She knew of no love affairs, no quarrel, she was sure he had no enemies. She guessed he would have had about £10 in his possession when he left. He had no worries financial or otherwise, money in the bank and invested in his name. A better boy never lived, industrious, upright, honourable and sober.

The only other witness was Henry Blendell of 38 High Street, Bolton, an employee at the tannery, who said he saw the deceased at 12.20 pm on 25th August with a suitcase. The analyst's report on the contents of the whisky bottle found by Walton showed it consisted of a few drops of water containing a small quantity of carbolic disinfectant, certainly not substantial enough if he meant it for suicide. However, the body was too decomposed to form any opinion of the cause of death.

At the end of the booklet Beatrice carefully ties up all these scattered threads, but this is a story which can only conclude with questions. Why did Walton come to remote and unknown Dartmoor, particularly to Postbridge where transport was not easy – how did he reach such a place? Where did he stay to change his suit? Where were the brown suit, raincoat and suitcase? Where was he from 25th August to 6th November, when did he die and from what cause? What connection was there between him and George Miller of Bolton found at the foot of Beachy Head? What is the significance of Walton's missing brown suit and George Miller's brown suit, and in each case of the left shoe and missing watch hand? Was the unidentified body on Dartmoor really that of Walton Howard?

So we come to the end of a tale which has no end.

Almost beyond Belief

Violent death – suicide or murder – leaves a shadow forever, especially when the reason for it is unsolved, as in the case of the Luxton Tragedy.

The ancient village of Winkleigh in Mid Devon stands on a lofty hill. It was founded by the Saxons in their early occupation of Devon, giving its name to a hundred. It has a small Norman castle site and at the southwestern end of Castle Street is a smaller mount known as Croft Castle. The tragedy took place at West Chapple Farm just outside this ancient village, where the lives of three members of a family who still lived virtually in a Victorian time warp ended when their dead bodies were found one September morning in 1975.

Frances, Robert and Alan Luxton, two brothers and a sister, were the last surviving members of a once rich, famous and widespread Devon family going back to the 14th century – gamblers, riders to hounds and landowners. But these three were recluses – in fact, the younger brother Alan had not been seen beyond the farm gate in 20 years. Recently little had been seen of the other two either. On the rare occasions they emerged in Winkleigh – always together – they were as emaciated as skeletons.

The family had been prominent in the district for centuries; they lived at the nearby manor of Holcombe in the 16th century, and Brushford Barton was a farm of 2,000 acres owned by the family since the reign of Elizabeth I. Other properties they owned were Hill Farm, Ridestone Farm, West Chapple and Higher Reve. Three farms in the area even took their names from there – Luxton Barton, East and West Luxton. The name was supposed to originate with a Winkleigh man called Lugg, a figure of some importance in the 13th century.

The 230 acre West Chapple farm had been worked with exactly the same equipment as the siblings' grandfather had used in the 19th century. Even in this secluded part of the county, yards and cowsheds had been concreted out on other farms, but here they were still paved or cobbled, the roofs of the buildings supported by beams which went back to medieval days, probably riddled with woodworm and dry rot. They used scythes to cut the crops and hay was turned with prangs or pitchforks, hedges were cut and layered in the old method which hardly anyone else in the county knew how to do, let alone spend precious man hours on the labour.

There was no gas, no mains electricity, and water power was provided by an enormous water wheel which stood in a wooden shed, a deep pit having been dug to insert it. Anyone who did not know the set up could have fallen 40 feet to the leat below. This wheel drove a Victorian thresher and crusher in the barns, fed by wooden culverts from a pond.

The house was lit by candles and paraffin lamps, which the family also carried out to the fields to inspect the cattle at night. A deserted house was used as a storage barn; this was Lute House and had been left to Alan in his father's will.

That is the backcloth of this drama – let us now look at the characters who acted out their horrific parts, reminiscent of Greek tragedy.

Apart from the three Luxtons, two labourers were employed on the farm. One, named Borowiez, was a Ukrainian refugee who had come to Britain after the war

West Chapple farmhouse and yard.

and ended up at Winkleigh in 1956. His accent was thick Eastern European overlaid with broad Devon, and he and his wife lived in a tied cottage at the entrance to the farm. The other man, Fred Lyne, and his wife lived in a terraced house in the village. He was a gentle, intelligent man who would be torn between shock and sorrow at the death of his employers, and bitterness at the way he'd been sacked with a week's notice and no compensation after having worked there all his life. He had been one of four men working there until the sister and two brothers took over. He said it was good land, but worked in the old fashioned way with out dated cattle and sheep – Ruby Reds and Longwools.

The main actors in the drama were Frances, Robert and Alan. Their father Robert John had married Wilmot Summerhayes in 1906, a dark eyed beauty who had been to a private school and also brought a small settlement with her.

She gave birth first to a daughter, which did not please Robert John – he needed boys to work on the farm. However, Frances grew up strong, red headed and pale skinned and worked as hard as any man.

Robert was born in 1911 and Alan ten years later. It was after his birth that Wilmot visibly aged and her health deteriorated. They were all brought up with strict discipline, particularly Frances whose sex her father resented. Daily he impressed upon them all the Luxton philosophy: 'You cannot take out more than you put in'. He never tired of telling them he was a yeoman farmer.

For Frances the day began at 6 am. Apart from farm and housework she helped to make cider in the ancient press and to process the rich milk into Devon clotted cream. The cider was part of the workers' pay – a common practice in Devon. In her childhood, dolls and other toys were unknown and there was always Robbie, her younger brother to look after. They went to school together, ate their lunch together, and his devotion to his sister became proverbial. She grew up with only scanty and strange notions of the world outside, she had never been to Exeter and had no idea of much beyond Mid Devon.

Robbie was sent to West Buckland School as a boarder, but after only two years his father took him away against the strong protests of the headmaster. He was needed to work in the fields.

Robbie grew more and more attached to Frances and dependent on her emotionally. A visiting cousin described how 'knowing' looks were exchanged between the two, saying he was aware of a more than brother and sisterly affection.

Meanwhile Frances longed to meet new people and travel. She joined the Devon County Dairy School in Crediton, and she taught herself to ride on an old brood mare called Tidy. Greatly daring and much to her father's annoyance, she actually went away for an eight day holiday to Scotland through a friend she had met at the Dairy School. The truth was her father had grown too ill to make much effort to object.

By now Robbie was 27 and following the pattern of his father's work. He was tough, energetic and ill tempered, totally reliant on Frances for his domestic and emotional comforts. Alan at 17 was morose and silent, working under his brother's orders. Neighbours noticed that Frances fussed over him and tried to give him plenty of her time for which he was not particularly grateful, and of course Robbie was jealous of him and taunted him by calling him 'Babe'.

By now both parents were sick and infirm with advancing years. Robert John died of pneumonia at the beginning of the war. In his will, in addition to Lute House, he left half of the farm to Alan – but it could not be sold without Robbie's agreement and the latter was determined life would go on as usual, the land would be farmed as it had always been.

Even in remote Devon the war touched the lives and land of the people. In the spring of 1940 a family of cockneys called Taylor came to Lute House as evacuees. This meant a trail of outsiders leaving gates open, stealing apples – but it was worst of all for Alan as it was his house. However, cashwise things brightened as the black market flourished in the area. In 1942 the United States built an airfield nearby and Alan, who was now in his late twenties and just ripe for some excitement, spent a lot of time in the King's Arms with the Yanks exchanging bacon, eggs, rabbits and so on, for cigarettes.

In 1944 the Americans were replaced by Canadians. It seems Frances met an airman called Mike McCallum but there is little known about the relationship.

By now Wilmot had died of cancer and as soon as the war was over life returned to its previous state. Robbie stuck to the way his father had farmed – the old routine, the old

The King's Arms, Winkleigh.

pattern. Still no tractor – draught horses pulled the plough or harrow.

Robbie also still treated Alan as an inferior, even buying his clothes and deducting the money from his wages. Rows started. Alan joined the Young Farmers' Club and took an interest in the Labour Party, making many friends in the village and beyond. He made lists of improvements to West Chapple including reconditioning Lute House where he proposed to live. However, Robbie was determined it should remain as a storage barn. Alan wanted to modernise the workload, bring in new breeds of cattle. The rows went on late into the night, becoming more physical. To try to keep the peace and enable him to get away from his brother, Frances bought Alan an old banger which he did up and drove around the countryside from Okehampton to Crediton and Exeter.

Lute House, Alan Luxton's property on the farm.

As for Frances, now in her forties, she had no social life, working all hours in the house, the garden, the fields. At one time she did manage to revolt against the daily grind and went to stay with a cousin in Highbury. There she met a well dressed, tough sailor who made her feel something she never had before – attractive, a woman. At the end of the week she returned to Devon. For a while they exchanged letters, perhaps they might have married, but eventually the whole thing died a natural death. The bond between herself and Robbie became even stronger.

In 1953 Alan asked Frances to lend him money to buy an engagement ring. His fiancee was Myrtle Standbury, a Winkleigh girl he had met through the Young Farmers. They were apparently much in love and it seemed a good match. He wanted to sell his share of the farm to Robbie and Frances and make a new life for himself, a fair enough request.

Robbie flatly refused, but he would agree to Lute House being renovated and they could continue as partners. Actually the way their father Robert John had left his will with restricting clauses was both unfair and cruel – Alan had no intention of continuing his partnership with his brother, their ideas on farming were diametrically opposed. He decided he would borrow the money and buy a cheap farm, using all the Government grants which were now available to update it.

The arguments went on night and day for weeks, starting at breakfast and going on outside well into the night. Frances refused to take sides. It was obvious Robbie was never going to give way, he loved the farm and the way of life – the status quo – with a passion and a conviction that he was right.

At last physical violence was involved. Alan walked about with a shotgun, and both Frances and one of the workmen tried to intervene. Alan broke off his engagement without any explanation. From then on he refused to eat or speak. His weight went down to eight stone, he was filthy and stinking, walking round with a sack tied round his waist.

Eventually Frances got the doctor and the social services and he was sent to Exeter as an in-patient at an asylum. When he returned to the farm his clothes were hanging on him, his bootlaces permanently untied. He talked and mumbled to himself, sometimes breaking out into abuse, shouting at the outside world. He needed Frances' permanent care and attention.

Now she was trying desperately to find cousins, relatives, someone, anyone to whom they could pass on the farm, to keep it in the family. She trailed round the churches and graveyards over half of Devon trying to trace them.

Suddenly with no explanation she went away in 1967. She was gone for three weeks and when she came back no one knew where she had been or what had happened, it was as though she had become a different person, something had changed her completely. She got Borowiez's wife to help clean, sprucing up not only the house, but herself. From then on each year she went away for several weeks. Surprisingly Robbie seemed to take it quite well – Alan simply stayed in bed talking to himself.

Then Robbie became ill, covered in some skin disease so that it was agony even to put on his boots. It was simply that there was too much work for too few hands, especially now Alan was useless and they were all getting older.

They decided the only thing to do was sell up, buy a small house and move into it. Frances found a place in Crediton. Now it was Alan who refused to co-operate, saying he would not give his permission to sell. However, the other two went ahead and some kind of arrangement was made – not exactly a contract but the shaking of hands on the deal. But even now Frances nearly drove the house agents mad by continually changing her mind, sometimes twice within one day. The problem as far as she was concerned was that the place in Crediton was too small, it would mean getting rid of most of their possessions from the past, and Frances simply could not bear to part with some of her treasures.

The sale was to be on Michaelmas Day . . . the last weeks of September came . . . nothing had been done about the move. . .

*　　*　　*

During the last week in September, Pearson Phillips wrote in the *Observer* a piece headed 'Tragic Farm Where Time Stood Still'.

The details which followed told how three members of the Luxton family of West Chapple Farm near Winkleigh in Mid Devon had been slaughtered. A story of crossed lovers, fights over property, a family feud ending in shattered bodies, it has a unique and chilling fascination set against the doom-ridden background of a remote farm which had no modern machinery, not even a tractor, and still no electricity or mains water.

A grocer's roundsman had called as usual at the farm early in the morning. He saw what he thought was a white scarecrow lying on the ground. The place seemed deserted except for a dog barking from a barn where it was obviously shut in. He got no answer to his knock on the back door. He went across the yard and it was then he saw that what he had thought was a bundle of rags was in fact a body above which hovered a cloud of flies.

He saw it was the body of Alan Luxton, the youngest of the family, dressed in pyjamas and army boots. The top part of his head was missing, the brains and part of the skull scattered far and wide as he lay in a pool of dark blood. There was no weapon near him.

The driver fled back for the police in the village. Within an hour Detective Chief Superintendent Proven Sharpe had set up investigations and a forensic expert was brought from Bristol by helicopter. As it was possible the killer was still at large they had to proceed with caution.

Moving round the yard, the garden and the orchard they found evidence of further deaths – flesh, bones, brains were widely scattered. The house was locked. There was no sign of either Robbie or Frances.

It was PC Tilke who found their corpses lying half hidden in the long grass of the orchard among the rotting apples. Frances' nightgown was pushed above her waist and she lay in an eerie position on all fours, her legs drawn up. The top of her head was missing, a large section of brain lay several feet from her body. Alongside was the body of her brother Robbie dressed in trousers, unlaced boots and a vest. He too had massive head injuries and several cuts through his cheek, lips, mouth and ears. An old shotgun lay by his side. In his pocket were unused and spent cartridges.

The bodies were removed to a mortuary in Exeter where Fred Lyne identified them. At the inquest Fred said he took his orders from the 'Maister' – Robbie. He described how Alan had walked around with a sack round him, varying in mood from madness to sanity. It had been soon after the discussions started over selling the house that he had seen Alan with the shotgun in his hands and suggested to Robbie he take it off him and hide the cartridges.

Mrs Borowiez gave evidence, saying she was a cleaner and often heard quarrelling. She was never allowed in the bedrooms where the three of them slept – cleaning was 'downstairs' only.

She said Frances had wanted to make a home for her brothers in this house in Crediton. Robbie admitted the farm had become too much for him, but Alan said if they went then he would stay on alone, which was of course ridiculous.

It is not hard to understand how these three felt: the farm had been in the family for generations, they had worked themselves to the bone to keep their home, now it was impossible. They shut themselves up in the house, like sick animals about to die. . . As in many Devonian families there was a history of cousins marrying cousins, often to keep money in the family, perhaps breeding mental instability. Frances had been obsessively interested in her family history. . . There were no Luxtons at the funeral.

At the inquest the Home Office Pathologist gave much detailed evidence regarding the gun and the method of shooting. The reason for Alan's brains being more widely scattered than those of the other two was that in the farming community suicides favoured the centre of the forehead for their target as in cattle with a humane killer. In summing up, the Coroner suggested that Robert and Frances had heard a shot, rushed from the house and found the body of their brother. In their deeply depressed state of mind, Robert shot his sister with or without her consent and then turned the gun on himself. So the verdict was that Alan Luxton committed suicide, Robert Luxton first killed his sister and then himself committed suicide.

No one will ever know what actually happened or can imagine the agony of mind those three suffered on that mild September morning under the apple trees, some heavy with fruit still. Trees that had produced cider for them down the generations and at whose feet now lay the last of the Luxton family.

THE GHOSTLY HIGHWAY

AN article in the *Sunday Express* in April 1979 described how a Mrs Davidson was driving home in the winter moonlight on a well known road near her home when suddenly the way ahead was no longer familiar – part of it blacked out, a road she had never seen before forked mistily away to her right. It seems nine people had died on that piece of carriageway in Kent since November 1977.

This brought vividly to mind the most famous of all mysteries to do with highways in Devon – that of the Hairy Hands.

Many roads in Devon are haunted by phantoms either visible or audible to many people. Usually there is a pervading aura of something tragic or evil which some say accounts for otherwise inexplicable accidents. Obviously of all these, those on Dartmoor roads must come top of the list. The atmosphere anyway is eerie, and it is easy enough to become disorientated in the low mist which often occurs. And there have been many unexplained incidents where the traveller sees or feels a huge pair of hairy hands interfering with handlebars or steering wheel.

So is there some kind of reserve of psychic power in the area? Is it simply a manifestation of force? In this case there does not seem to be any mention of it before the second decade of the 20th century. Perhaps it is the presence of some malignant influence or matter which once created can never be destroyed – neither of the human nor of the spirit world but earthbound between the two, freed from the body but not from the scene of some crime committed during life on this earth.

Perhaps violent death and emotions can leave imprints on the ether, concentrated with such force as to form definite emanations. Is this more far fetched than imagining what effect it would have had on a prehistoric man if he had seen a personality on a television screen, appearing out of a box, which is something we take as perfectly normal today.

These particular happenings occur between Postbridge and Two Bridges in the Archerton region of the Moor. Only once was I frightened in this spot, when I got enveloped in a typical Dartmoor mist, thick and obliterating so that I suddenly felt a complete isolation in time and place. Perhaps it was the utter silence after the constant racket we live in today, but there is a very narrow margin between loneliness and plain fear. I only know that now I avoid that place on my own.

This area became of interest to the general public in the early 1920s. In 1921 there were three motoring accidents near the gate of Archerton Drive on Nine Mile Hill, reported in the *Daily Mail* on 14th and 15th October. The first had been in March when Dr Helby, the prison doctor from Princetown, had been asked to attend an inquest at Postbridge. He was riding a bike with a sidecar containing two children, daughters of the Deputy Governor of the prison, and his own wife, Mrs Helby. Suddenly the machine swerved, the engine literally detaching itself as he was flung into the ditch and his neck broken. The children and his wife fell on the verge and were not seriously hurt but naturally terrified.

Having written an account of this, I had a letter from a Dr Adkin of Exmouth. He told me that when he was a small boy he and his family were staying on holiday at

Cherrybrook Farm, now a hotel. (By kind permission of Nick Wotton)

Cherrybrook Farm near to Archerton not far from where the old powder mill and buildings still stand, and recalled this incident well.

They were passing a small gravel pit dug out by the road men to repair potholes before the days of tarmac – the family were on their way to their holiday cottage on the farm. There were signs of an accident a little way ahead and his father, a doctor, telling his family to stay where they were, went to see if he could help.

He realised immediately that the man was dead. He managed to get some words out of the wife, who said that as they approached the place where the accident occurred her husband had cried out that he had lost control of the machine and something about 'hair' and 'hands' which made no sense.

A few weeks later a motor coach mounted the bank on the Lake side of the road and one woman was badly hurt. The driver said, 'I felt hands pull the wheel towards the Lake side', but no one listened to him.

Later that year, on a dull, foggy Friday – 26th August – an Army officer was riding a motor bike and was again thrown on the verge in exactly the same place. He only suffered shock and scratches but he was a very experienced rider. He said, 'It was just not my fault, something seemed to wrench me off the road, a huge hairy pair of hands closed over mine on the handlebars. I tried to fight them but they were too strong'.

As all these stories gradually gained prominence, the *Daily Mail* sent investigators to the spot and their report appeared that October. Eventually the camber of the road was altered, but it made no difference and in any case all these vehicles had turned over upwards to the Lake side,

The Ghostly Highway. (By kind permission of Nick Wotton)

both the coach and the officer's cycle travelling uphill.

Forty years later, in 1961 a young man was driving from Plymouth to Chagford when his car overturned on exactly the same spot. He was found dead underneath it. In spite of a thorough examination of the body by forensic experts, and of the mechanism of the car, no explanation of the accident could be given.

In 1991 a doctor from Somerset turned his car over at the same place. He said, like the others, it was as if some malignant force had sent it out of control. The atmosphere inside the car was deathly cold, literally paralysing him. He shook all over and again said, 'It was as if something evil was actually inside the car with me, the steering wheel went wild and was wrenched out of my hands'.

Someone else who knew much about this drama was Theo Brown, that expert on all to do with folklore, mystery and ghosts in Devon. She told me what a Mrs Battiscombe had described to her; she was the widow of the successor to the prison doctor from Princetown who had been killed.

'A young man who was a guest at Penlee in Postbridge undertook to run in to Princetown on his motorbike to get something for his hostess,' she said. 'In about an hour he returned to Penlee very white and shaken saying he had had a most frightening experience. He had felt his hands gripped by two rough and hairy hands which made every effort to throw him off his machine. He never got much beyond the clapper bridge.'

Theo's own parents knew the area very well, for a month each summer they used to park a caravan among the old ruins of the powder mill a mile west of Postbridge, half a mile north of the haunted road.

One night when the family were asleep in their bunks in the caravan Theo had woken up with a promonition of danger. Suddenly she was wide awake and looking up at the little window above her bunk she saw fingers and the palm of a very large hand with hairs on it – it was clawing at the top of the window which was a little way open.

'I had the feeling that the owner of the hand was about to harm us – it was no human hand.' She made the sign of the cross and prayed to God to keep them from harm. Slowly the hand sank down the window out of sight. They stayed on for the rest of the holiday but she never felt any evil near the caravan again.

One curious fact about these hauntings is that four of the people affected in accidents were doctors, including Dr Helby, Dr Adkin senior who helped at the accident, and his son, Dr Adkin, who had written to me although only a child at the time. The latter did not mention in his letter whether he had ever driven along this piece of road since. Perhaps he had felt discretion was the better part of valour! Number four was the doctor from Somerset whose name we do not know. Possibly this spirit, ghost or whatever, had a special grudge against the medical profession for some reason.

As I write, it is some years since there have been any reports of 'happenings' here but, as I said before, it is not a place I would walk alone.

To end with, an evocative poem written by Nick Wotton, a great lover of, and expert guide to, Dartmoor – who also took the photographs.

THE HAIRY HANDS OF DARTMOOR

To drive across the cold grey road
From Princetown, in the night
Take care to keep your windows closed
Make sure the steering wheel's held tight
For years ago from nowhere
As many a folk will tell
The hairy hands would follow you
And all would not be well

As winter storms rolled over Dartmoor
The grazing stock would hide
For to travel east to Postbridge
At your peril you would ride
At the Cherrybrook the water's crossed
By a granite bridge of stone
It would be wise at this strange old spot
Not to dwell alone

There under the towering tors
That peer down from the moor
Stories of hairy hands
From days not long before
A chilled feeling in the atmosphere
Could fill your car with fear
The wheel you held would tighten
When the bridge became quite near

Some victims of this experience
Insist the story's real
They all agree that hairy hands
Had gripped their steering wheel
We shall never know the reason
For this Dartmoor mystery
This phenomenon has ceased it seems
At last the trapped is free.

THE LONELY SEA
AND THE SKY

THE poet Masefield said all he fancied was 'a tall ship and star to sail her by'. But as more and more men and women make the oceans of the world seem smaller by their wonderful conquests in time and speed, do we who at best venture out on a calm day with its cloudless blue skies, in a dinghy, cabin cruiser or yacht, really know what it is like to be totally alone on a vast sea? Perhaps in a storm which seems to go on forever, determined in the destruction of both the vessel and ourselves, perhaps when all contact with other human beings has broken down?

It needs the kind of person who can suffer their own company for months on end, whose mind is conditioned to swift and correct decision in an emergency and who has not taken on a task which in his heart he knows is beyond him. Perhaps above all, a person who can come to terms with their own character in the ultimate loneliness and danger that thousands of miles of empty sea can offer.

It must have been obvious to everyone that this was no description of Donald Crowhurst. And yet he had persuaded even his wife, Clare, that he would achieve not only the completion of the course but would win The *Sunday Times* Golden Globe Race to be sailed single-handed, non-stop round the world.

On an October morning in 1968 his friends and a BBC

cameraman watched as Donald left Teignmouth harbour in the trimaran *Teignmouth Electron* – and so began the extraordinary events surrounding this strange voyage with a tragic ending as mysterious and unsolved as that of the *Mary Celeste*. He only had hours to spare before the deadline to prepare everything, in fact even as we and the BBC cameras watched him being towed out of the harbour it appeared that the sails were attached to the wrong halyards – just another of the difficulties which had dogged the whole project.

Soon we listened to radio reports (no satellites in 1968). We scanned the papers and for a fortnight no messages were received from *Electron*. It seemed she must be making poor progress.

Eventually on 15th November a message came from off Portugal saying he had logged 1,300 miles, but only 800 of these were on his route – already he was having trouble with the generator.

On 10th December he was making better progress and claimed to have made a record 243 miles in one day. The press was over the moon – a possible winner. . .

Other entrants such as Chay Blyth and John Ridgway had dropped out, Carozzo of Italy had retired with a stomach ulcer, Robin Knox-Johnson's boat *Suhaili*, the oldest and smallest entry, had been badly battered off New Zealand. Nigel Tetley had broken the record to the Cape for a multihull but with Crowhurst making such splendid time it seemed the vision of him as a winner was far from unlikely, despite the difficulties he had had before setting off.

The positions Crowhurst gave were somewhat vague; it seemed as if he was in the Indian Ocean but by March 1969 he had narrowed the distance between himself and Tetley. It had been thought Knox-Johnson had been lost round the Horn but actually he too was back in the race which seemed to have developed between the two trimarans of Tetley and

Donald Crowhurst on board 'Teignmouth Electron'. (By kind permission of Teignmouth Museum)

Crowhurst. The latter's messages now suggested he was near Diego Ramirez south of the Horn.

On 21st May Tetley's boat sank. It was just a formality for Crowhurst to pick up the prize, all he had to do was reach home.

At Teignmouth preparations were made for his eventual return. The BBC and ITV would record his escorted return up channel, the firms who had given him supplies prepared their advertisements. On 18th June the BBC sent congratulations and asked him to have films and tapes ready. On 25th June *Teignmouth Electron* was sighted by a Norwegian cargo ship; Crowhurst waved, apparently fit and cheerful.

On 26th June Donald received a message from his press agent to the effect that the *Daily Express* and his wife were

Clare and Donald Crowhurst. (By kind permission of Teignmouth Museum)

meeting him off the Scillies, while 100,000 people were waiting to welcome him in Teignmouth.

Cheerfully he radioed back his position. People were a little surprised he insisted his wife should not come out to meet him but the press covered this with excuses that he would be busy repairing some of the broken gear, that he would be worn out by the long struggle . . . only Clare, his wife, was now concerned how the world trip would have affected him.

From then on nothing was heard. On the morning of 10th July 1969 the Royal Mail vessel *Picardy* bound from London to the Caribbean sighted a small yacht cruising along slowly with only a mizzen sail raised. The time was 7.50 am. It was 1,800 miles out in the Atlantic, a most unlikely place to find a small sailing yacht.

The Chief Officer, Joseph Clark, roused the Master, Captain Box, from his bunk. There was no one on the yacht's deck. They altered course to pass round her stern and sounded the foghorn three times. The name on the bow was *Teignmouth Electron* of Bridgwater. The name rang a bell connected with the Golden Globe Race. Perhaps someone was ill? Box stopped his engines and lowered a boat, and with a crew of three Clark investigated.

The yacht was deserted. The cabin was a mess with unwashed dishes in the sink, two of the three radio receivers were in pieces, a dirty sleeping bag lay on the floor. Food and water seemed adequate. The only thing missing was the chronometer from its case. A life raft was firmly lashed to its place on deck, sails neatly folded, nothing to indicate what had happened. Three log books were piled on the chart table, methodically kept – the last entry in the radio log was 29th June.

On 10th July Captain Box radioed London that Donald Crowhurst had vanished. As soon as Rodney Hallworth, Donald's publicity agent, heard that the log books were intact he sold the copyright to the *Sunday Times* for £4,000. A group was organised to fly out and collect them.

Captain Box met them with the news that on reading the logs he had found something seriously wrong. . .

To understand this extraordinary, unsolved mystery we must look at the man, Donald Crowhurst, in some detail, and study the progress of the voyage.

He was born in India in 1932. His father John was a highly intelligent man with the prestigious position of a superintendent on the railways. He had a slight tendency to drink rather heavily at times. His wife was a school teacher and young Donald was known as brave and very self confident.

When the partition of India came John brought his family back to England. In 1947 Donald went to Loughborough College, but had to leave as soon as he had taken his school certificate as his parents were finding life in England very different from India, both socially and financially.

John died in 1948. Donald joined the RAF, got a commission, learned to fly at Farnborough and studied electronics. Now being better off he bought a Lagonda sports car in which he was inclined to show off and got into several scrapes which led to his dismissal, but this did not stop him joining the Army, where once again he proved to be slapdash and irresponsible.

He had tried for one of the Cambridge Universities, but failed Latin in the first exam. He now settled down to working on electronics at Reading University and in 1957 he met his wife Clare at a party.

This was the year he bought the 20 foot sloop which he called *Pot of Gold* and took up sailing seriously. For a short time he had a job at Mullards, an electrical components firm, but he crashed the firm's car and that was the end of that.

It seemed at 26 years old most of the things he had tried had failed, but while he was working for a firm at Bridgwater he designed a radio direction finding device that he called 'Navicator' for yacht navigation. With this he set up his own business which he called Electron Utilisation, based in Bridgwater.

One of his chief failings seemed to be lack of control of his own intellect, even making faults in simple mathematics and being generally slapdash. With his passion for cars he had bought a new Jaguar which he drove with his usual *élan* – too fast – and had a bad crash, injuring his head and resulting in something of a personality change, making him moody.

Looking round for support for his venture he met Stanley Best who became his backer. Best was a first class businessman but he soon found his partner left much to be desired; whilst he was a brilliant innovator he was hopeless from the business and organising side. He simply saw things as he wanted them to be. Oddly enough, in some strange way Best seemed almost to come under his spell. Undoubtedly Donald's often misplaced but convincing enthusiasm was catching, giving him a kind of charisma.

In 1966/7 Francis Chichester, later to be knighted, made his solo round-the-world voyage. Immediately it became Donald's obsession to do exactly the same; he probably thought the publicity it would bring would help to save his now ailing firm. Meanwhile Chichester's success had engendered great interest among the general public and the *Sunday Times* had decided to sponsor a race to be called The Golden Globe, a single-handed non-stop race around the world with a prize of £5,000, with starting dates between 1st June and 31st October 1968. With his enormous self assurance Donald suggested he 'borrow' *Gypsy Moth IV* for a year and enter the race. The idea was firmly rejected owing to his lack of sailing experience. As it happened, Sir Francis was highly suspicious of him from the start.

Although he had no boat, in character Donald declared himself a race competitor, having persuaded Stanley Best to finance the building of a trimaran by Cox Marine Ltd of Brightlingsea, Essex, completed by LJ Eastwood of Brumhall in Norfolk. Best's wife was horrified and told her husband he was crazy. He admitted Donald was the most impressive and convincing of men – perhaps plausible would have been a better word, for he gave Best the impression he was being sponsored elsewhere and if anything went wrong the firm of Electron Utilisation would buy the boat.

It was at this time with the yacht under consideration that Crowhurst met Rodney Hallworth, ex-crime reporter and proprietor of the Devon News Agency. He lived in Teignmouth where he was Public Relations Officer to the Teignmouth Town Council. He persuaded Crowhurst to start and finish the race at Teignmouth and to name the yacht *Teignmouth Electron*, thereby bringing much-needed publicity to the town.

The completed boat eventually sailed to Teignmouth on 23rd September for final preparations by Morgan-Giles boatyard, there being only a month left before the latest permissable departure date on 31st October. The terms of entry were that competitors did not have to make a formal application, they could start where and when they liked so long as it was between the specified dates and that their departure and arrival were recorded by a national newspaper or magazine.

Another trimaran had been entered by Nigel Tetley, upon whose design Donald's boat was based. One of the faults of a trimaran was its tendency to remain upside down if it capsized, but full of confidence Donald said he had invented an electronic system which would not only give warning signals of unusual stresses but would right the vessel by means of a computer. As it happened he had not even designed it yet but true to character he affirmed all the time that he had no doubts about winning this race.

One day Donald had been asked, 'What would you do if you failed to get the boat down the Atlantic to the Southern ocean?' His reply was typical, 'Well, one could always shuttle around in the South Atlantic for a few months. There are places south of the shipping lanes where no one would ever spot a boat like this.' Jokingly, on their map he traced a course around the Falkland Islands and Tristan da Cunha. Everyone thought it was a great joke.

The BBC and ITV had bought the tape and recording rights, supplied a camera and tape recorder. At the boatyard there was still much to do to make the yacht ready. Time was running out but typically Donald swung from panic at the amount still to be done, to full confidence. Actually even at this early stage the BBC man in charge of the cameras began to suspect they might be shooting not for a triumph but for a disaster of some kind. On the eve of the departure he stopped filming, making an excuse to help stow some of the gear.

Although Donald's wife was aware the project was unlikely to be a success unfortunately his own supreme confidence again misled her. She could not know that he hoped she would beg him to back out, which he could then have done for family reasons – but she was unaware of his growing misery and self doubt and only tried to encourage him.

He left with just nine hours to spare and with the cabin and deck in untidy chaos. Instead of following the usual routine used on such an occasion – once their boat was clear of the harbour a contestant in such a race would drop anchor to clear up, check equipment and instruments – Donald headed straight for Cape Finisterre.

On 15th November, off Portugal, having logged 1,300 miles he was actually only 800 miles along the specified route, a distance he intended to cover in six days. He began

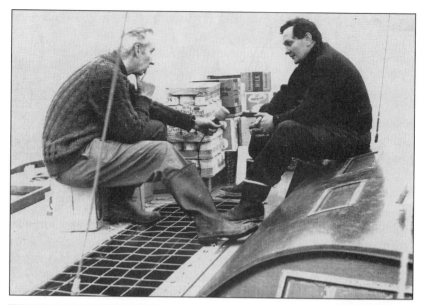

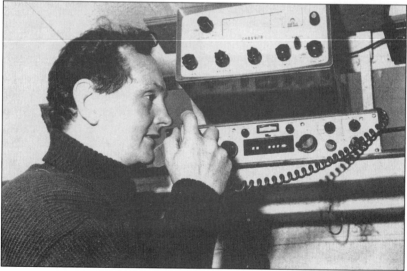

Crowhurst talking to a BBC reporter (top) and in radio contact. (By kind permission of Teignmouth Museum)

to realise there was no way in which he could win the race at such a slow pace.

It was when he reached the Canary Islands he actually contemplated the deception which, eight months later, Captain Box was to discover as he read the log books. And it was when he was off Cape Verde Island on 6th December he started the false route.

On 19th December he crossed the equator, on 26th December he was off Brazil when he found damage to the starboard hull. It was about a fortnight later he started radio silence, said to be due to generator problems once more.

One can only surmise his state of mind, confined to a tiny cabin. The steering gear, which had also given trouble, was shedding screws and he took replacements for these from other parts of the boat, which was leaking. His radio contact broke down continuously. Several times the thought of dropping out altogether must have crossed his mind, but how could he after all his boasting? So the two log books came into being, one true and one false.

When he got the radio working again he listened in to broadcasts from other ships in various positions so he could record false weather conditions.

On 6th March he sailed into Rio Salado in Argentina to make repairs but landed on a sand bank – of course this would have disqualified him if the race organisers got to hear of it. A couple of coastguards gave him a hand. One had telephoned La Planta Prefecture to ask for permission; a young midshipman answered the message, he didn't even consider it important enough to inform his seniors. For once Donald's luck was in, but perhaps it was this contact at last with human beings after being alone for so long that was the last straw. He was suffering from the strain of telling lies, the false log and now this fear of his landing being discovered, so he sailed further south in the hope of shooting pictures of the Horn to act as proof he had been around it.

By 29th March he was off the Falkland Islands after meandering slowly round the South Atlantic. Then turning north he broke radio silence at last to send false signals about his position. By 4th May his false route would now have taken him to a position where he could restart serious racing and cease deception.

On 21st May when Nigel Tetley's boat sank it put Crowhurst apparently in the lead. All this time his log books were filled with strange entries as despair over his situation increased. His mind seemed to be breaking down. The sinking of Tetley was the supreme irony, for if Donald won his log books would be carefully inspected and he would be exposed as a cheat, whereas if he had come in second there would be no need to scrutinise the logs and he would have been hailed as a hero for his accomplishments.

On 23rd June the last entry was made in the navigation log. The other log books were filled with such quotations as, 'I see what I am and I see the nature of my offence . . . it is finished – it is finished IT IS THE MERCY. . .' There were pleas for forgiveness.

He removed the line he normally streamed astern as a precaution against falling overboard. He stopped writing at 11.18 am sometime after 29th June. It can then only be presumed he picked up the chronometer and stepped off the stern of the boat into the sea.

Whatever we may think of him, whatever else he may have been, Donald Crowhurst was neither a fool nor a villain. In fact Captain Craig Rich, lecturer at the School of Navigation, who was advising the race organisers and had examined the log books said the fact he had sailed over 16,000 miles single-handed must at least be considered a remarkable achievement in itself. The real tragedy of the whole affair did not spring from lack of skill or physical courage but from the fact that he didn't have the moral courage to admit he had made a mistake and that he lacked

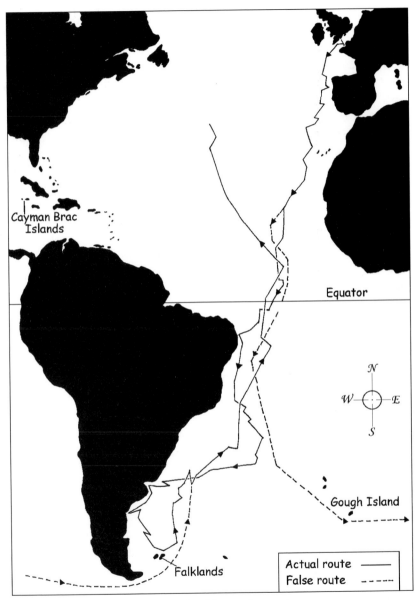

Crowhurst's voyage, showing the false and actual routes.

the mental stability necessary for a long distance solitary sailor. All his life he was able to convince others of his own ability because he convinced himself of it and people believed in and supported him.

The truth could not be suppressed, it was decided to publish the full account. Clare and the BBC had to be told. The latter were already preparing the story of Crowhurst's 'heroic' voyage; only the Director General knew the reason for the programme being put on hold.

From the evidence of the log books it was presumed he had committed suicide, although some of his friends said he was prone when preoccupied to become clumsy and had actually fallen overboard during navigational tests on several occasions. Perhaps that is what happened, who knows.

As for the *Teignmouth Electron*, she can still be seen where she lies rotting on the small island of Cayman Brac in the West Indies.

The Unsolved Mysteries of Pinkworthy Pool

FACT is so often more sinister and more mysterious than any fiction thought up by a writer's imagination. On the day I went to find the source of the River Exe for a feature on that river the backdrop could not have been more apt. The July day was overcast and heavy with the threat of distant thunder and the irritating buzz of enormous flies. Silence brooded over Exmoor as though the world had ceased to turn on its axis.

Here is the head of the valley of Lorna Doone where the hump of Chains Barrow swells up – certainly the most lonely and desolate spot on the whole moor. The mire at my feet eventually became a wide stream running under the river's first bridge: Exe Head Bridge.

To be honest I had never heard of Pinkworthy Pool until I started to study the map in detail. The name – rather fanciful, romantic, almost childlike – seemed a most unlikely description for anything in these surroundings and the more I repeated it the more it fascinated me, as did the inexplicable atmosphere of evil. Abandoning my original purpose I decided to explore its history.

It was quite obvious this was no natural formation, but I found it difficult to understand why anyone should have created this overgrown pond in such a place. I discovered it was the creation of Sir John Knight in the early 19th century,

The first bridge over the River Exe at Exe Head.

and that it is the highest sheet of water in England south of the Pennines, covering three acres.

John was an ironmaster from the Midlands, who had bought and reclaimed the land in this area which was once the old Royal Forest. He created a dozen farmsteads which he rented out to tenants to encourage them to improve the moorland with grass and root crops, mainly for sheep which are still the lifeblood of Exmoor. Basically his plan is still carried out with the hill farming of today.

For a moment let us look at the formation of the pond as it will have quite a bearing on the story later. It was dug out by hand in those days by 200 Irish labourers, with two 9 foot outlet pipes which were plugged with two enormous pieces of good English oak. These were situated above each other on the pool side of the dam wall. To reach them there was a tunnel 60 yards long and under 3 feet in height in some places, a difficult place to search for bodies, as became necessary on two occasions.

In March 1889 Mr and Mrs William Gammon lived at Rowley Barton not far from Parracombe. She died when she was 50, however there was nothing particularly sinister about this. They had been married for many years, a most devoted couple and many people said he never recovered from this tragic loss.

However, after some little time he began to find solace elsewhere with a woman a few years younger than himself. At first she was flattered by his attentions, but as it turned out she did not want to be tied to an older man. William's offer was perfectly genuine, no doubt he felt extremely lonely without a close companion after so many years.

Eventually she told him there was no point in continuing the relationship, which she then broke off. This turn of events – losing his wife and now this rejection – he could not handle. His personality changed to such an extent that he refused to seek help or discuss the matter with anyone. In those days if you had troubles you got on with life with the help of your own family, not outsiders. William had no one he could unburden his sorrow upon.

Suddenly he disappeared.

A few days later someone walking near Pinkworthy Pool, probably looking for a lost sheep, came upon William's pony cropping the short turf. This was certainly a little distance from the farm and it seemed strange if he had been thrown and could not remount that the pony had not returned to its stable with an empty saddle. Most curious of all, leading to gossip, as can be imagined, his clothes, neatly folded were found on the edge of the pool. Immediately a wide search was set up over the moor. The only clue was that he had told the woman who had rejected him that he 'intended to visit Pinkworthy'. Whether there was something sinister behind this, as it was said shortly before the event, no one will ever know.

At this time of year it was bitterly cold on the moor. It was certain he could not survive for long with no clothes, particularly if he had either fallen or jumped into the icy water.

A diver was sent for, who made several attempts to explore the muddy water without success. It must have been dark as night in the depths.

Eventually it was decided the only course was to drain the pool. This meant removing the two plugs referred to earlier, which involved men having to go down the tunnel. Fortunately for them it was not long before they discovered the corpse of William Gammon. Many questions arose from this discovery. Why did he take off all his clothes if he was about to commit suicide? Does someone with such an act in mind fold their clothes in a neat pile? It could hardly be thought that he had chosen that bitter weather simply to go for a swim. There was no alternative but a verdict of suicide at the inquest.

Most likely the woman with whom he had formed a fairly close relationship, indeed sufficient to ask her to marry him, got a great deal of criticism for not thinking it odd that he had used the phrase he did about the Pond. Although not all that distant on horseback, there was no apparent reason for the journey.

Twenty three years passed, and then in 1912 the mystery was again revived because there had been another and far more bizarre disappearance in the neighbourhood.

The Stenner family lived at White Cross just outside the village of Exford. William, the man of the house, was 41, a farm labourer, and he and his wife had six children. They were a devoted and united family. He was well known as a conscientious worker and to everyone in the village their way of life, though hard, seemed content with no particular worries.

So it is odd that in August of that year he should tell his wife he was having serious problems in sleeping. To me this seems a strange fact because, bearing in mind the period and that they were country folk, it is very unlikely that they would have had separate beds even, let alone separate bedrooms so surely she would have realised this without being told. It also appears he had not mentioned it to anyone else. For a time, she said, she was worried, but normally William was a healthy, strong, steady person and so her worry did not last for long. It was probably just a temporary setback – indigestion perhaps.

However, he then acted out of character by going to bed one night very early saying he felt physically exhausted. For a moment she was surprised, she could never remember his admitting to such a thing before. However, she finished clearing the supper things, put the kettle back on the stove and went upstairs to see if he would like a cup of tea.

She crept very quietly into the room and saw he was still awake. She told him the kettle was on the boil, he said he would very much like a cup of tea, perhaps it would help him to sleep.

She made a pot, poured two cups and went back up the stairs. To her surprise the bed was empty, the clothes pushed back. She called his name and started to search the house. Perhaps it was just a joke, he was hiding from her. Eventually she went back to the bedroom but there was no sign of him. She even looked under the bed and opened the wardrobe door; all his clothes were there. He could not possibly have got out of the house because he would have had to pass her to reach the door.

It was then she noticed the window was open at the bottom, from where it was only a slight drop to the soft grass. She ran over and looked out. No sign. Nothing was missing except the nightshirt he had put on to go to bed, not even a pair of shoes or slippers.

She ran to the village – the search started. As is often the way in the month of August on the moor, the weather can turn cold and windy with rain lashing the countryside like winter, making crossing it almost an impossibility. However, the search carried on.

And so did the wagging tongues. However much a family is respected, perhaps even more so when they are – the story is more juicy – everyone takes a delight in surmising what the details can be.

Where on earth could he have gone? Had he run away to a secret mistress he had kept carefully from his wife and everyone else all these years? Had they made a well organised arrangement to elope? Most of the men thought William had perhaps incurred debts beyond his means and either his creditors or the bank were increasing their demands for settlement, and he simply disappeared to get out of their clutches, but the police could find nothing suspicious in his financial affairs, nor any trace of a relationship which could have solved the mystery. It was as if he had simply melted into thin air – had never existed.

The two Masters of the local fox and stag hunts were of enormous help searching in the deep hidden areas of the moor which they knew well from hunting over it, and where it would have been possible to hide a body.

The search continued all through the winter, the deep snow and bitter gales. By the turn of the year it became the general opinion that there was only one place where they had not made a thorough search and, remembering the bloated body of another William, it was decided once more to drag Pinkworthy Pool.

This meant again using the tunnel and removing the plug from the top pipe. This went badly wrong during the operation making the water deeper than ever, and with all the prodding and activity a deep layer of thick mud was disturbed and turned the water black.

Some kind of platform was erected down the tunnel. An hydraulic jack was brought in and stood on the platform but as the men worked on trying to release the plug the platform collapsed and they were lucky not to be killed as the whole thing crashed into the tunnel.

At last they did succeed and as the water gushed through they managed to scramble out of danger. By now a huge crowd had assembled expecting to see the body of William Stenner, but although every nook and cranny, every small pool was searched in the area there was no sign of a body and once more Pinkworthy was filled with water.

So now the rumours started up again. It was assumed he had left the area, once more the questions of money or a woman became the forefront of gossip. His wife must have suffered greatly from the cruel remarks and insinuations both she and the children at school were subjected to.

Six months later interest was starting to flag when on a February afternoon Reg Hookway comes innocently into the picture. He was a farm labourer and his boss had sent him to

Muddicombe to check on some cattle. He walked along the White Post road and came to an old house and ruined buildings about 400 yards from the Stenners' house. The ruins stood where a mine had once been in use, the crumbling shaft still standing on the site closed many years ago.

Fascinated by the eerie amosphere, or perhaps just naturally with a young man's curiosity, he peered down into the deep blackness of the opening. As his eyes grew accustomed to the gloom he could see something white lying a little way down. Perhaps it was a stray cow or sheep that had fallen down and died, they did sometimes as these shafts had no fencing round them. He had brought a hay fork with him and he lent down trying to shift the object. He nearly fell down to join it when he realised it was the body of a human being – a man dressed in what remained of a white nightshirt.

Dropping the fork in terror he ran back to the village. The problem now arose of getting the body out as the entrance to the mine shaft was only two feet wide and was behind a large fallen boulder. However, a couple of men managed to squeeze behind this and raised the body from the freezing water. At once they recognised William Stenner, whose corpse had been preserved in the icy conditions.

During the original search all of Muddicombe including the mine shaft had been checked and there had definitely been no body there at the time. Could it have been that as it was so near the Stenners' house the search had not been quite so thorough here as elsewhere?

But none of this answered the mystery of why William had left his home through a bedroom window in a nightshirt. There had been no sign of a struggle, he must have gone of his own free will – it was odd too that he should have retired to bed so early, an almost unknown occurrence.

To everyone it seemed the most likely conclusion was murder, but he would have had to be overcome at once or he would have had time to shout for his wife. Had this been a fictional crime story it would probably have turned out that Mrs Stenner was having an affair and had a rural 'contract' on her husband's life so she could go to her lover. It is logical too that she helped in the general search for him to begin with, so she knew which areas had been covered and which had not. Then it would be safe for the body to be put down the mineshaft.

Today a clever lawyer would say it was very odd that such a devoted wife had not noticed her husband's depression which was so out of character. An interesting point I noticed in my research, though no one commented on this, is that with the help of an accomplice she could have killed William during the afternoon if the house was empty, which of course we do not know. Together her lover and she, and perhaps some other person, could have hidden the body temporarily and then moved it to the mine, or even put it there in the first place when the water might have been higher, covering it so that whoever searched that particular area would not have seen it if they had not bothered to squeeze behind the boulder. But if that were so, why had she not joined her lover? Perhaps they both lost their nerve, knowing it would be too obvious and even more intense enquiries would be made? But there is no one to confirm her story and we still have the fact that her husband behaved completely out of character with apparently no cause.

So here are two strange deaths about which we shall never know the truth, and Pinkworthy in spite of its sugary name played a part in both sinister cases. No wonder it has this aura hanging over it and I was glad to return to the busy village of Exford where the happy laughter and shouts of children playing on the banks of the river echoed now that afternoon school was over.

Maybe they were descendants of William Stenner . . . or even William Gammon.

'Out of the Very Mouth of Babes. . .'

D URING the whole of the enquiry the main witness stood quietly in the court and answered all the questions he was asked in a clear and straightforward manner.

'I was with Mr Baker on Saturday evening when I went to the field with the bullocks,' he explained. 'I saw Albert shoot Mr Baker. I saw Albert up on Mr Luscombe's field hedge with the gun and go out over. Albert fired the gun at Mr Baker and I saw him bleeding from the face. I saw Albert fire the gun the second time. He got off the hedge and ran after Mr Baker and shot while both were running. I saw Mr Baker fall down the first time after Albert fired and then got up and ran away towards the gate, and fell down where he was found. I saw Mr Baker bleeding and he had to walk with his head down.'

A juryman interrupted with a question but Mr Kellock, the deputy coroner in charge, said the witness was giving evidence splendidly. 'Let him alone to tell his own story.'

The witness continued, 'After Mr Baker fell down the second time Albert ran back through the hedge and into the next field. I ran down to tell Mrs Cummings what had happened and met her coming up.'

That was the testimony of Wilfred Perrott aged 5½ years, who was propped between the knees of his father, Mr J. S. Perrott.

It was certainly unusual for such a young child to give witness, but there was another extraordinary feature about this double tragedy of murder and suicide. In defence, the father of the man who had committed this crime said his son had been stung by a viper nine years ago, and on each anniversary since then his face had gone into spasms that were so hideous and uncontrollable that he had to turn away from the stares of anyone who saw him. This had made him somewhat anti-social for which he was not responsible, nor for his action at the time. Whether this was the anniversary to which he referred I could find no confirmation.

The coroner remarked that the bite or sting of a viper would not have any effect after nine years.

Kingsbridge, where the inquest on Hubert Baker and Albert Corner was held.

The accounts of the crime were given in the local papers in the South Hams on 18th June 1904. The inhabitants of Kingsbridge and the surrounding area were so shocked that on the Sunday many of them walked out to the scene of the tragedy – Warcombe Farm, two miles from the town.

Cars were few on the road in those days and the man who had broken the news to the police was Mr Edward Friend, who had gone a hard gallop on his chestnut mare down Fore Street. He was a horsebreaker who lived in the small hamlet of Ledstone near Kingsbridge. Albert Corner, the murderer and suicide, was aged 20, a farm apprentice.

It seems Corner had been 'paid off' or sacked by his employer, Mr Hubert Baker aged 28. His revenge for this was to shoot Baker dead; he had then cleared off with a stolen gun. Police Sergeant Yendell, in fine style like the Canadian Mounties, saddled up his and rode out from Kingsbridge. All this drama was rather spoilt later when it

Ledstone Farm, home of Edward Friend who reported the murder.

was reported that he was actually a first class bike rider and it was that machine he had used – already saddled!

Two other policemen had also been alerted and arrived on the scene where Dr de Courcey had pronounced the victim dead. It was known that Albert Corner was a man of violent and uncertain temper and now he was at large with a lethal weapon. However, the search was short as they found his body in a field about 100 yards away from Baker where he had apparently turned the gun on himself.

Albert was the fourth son of a tanner, William Corner who lived at Goveton near Ledstone. The family were somewhat looked upon as 'incomers' as they came from Mid Devon. He had had several jobs on local farms but because of the violence of his temper and a dour manner he never got on with his fellow labourers. He had worked for Mr Luscombe of Rake but he was so insolent and surly that he had been dismissed.

Hubert Baker on the other hand was well known and respected in the area, a man who loved his way of life as a farmer. His widowed sister Mrs Cummings was his housekeeper, to whom he was very attached, saying he would never marry as long as she could go on looking after him – he could not wish for better. And actually it was known locally that he had no particular woman friend. He had no enemy either, no evil was ever spoken of him and this terrible act was simply revenge exacted by a youth whom it appeared Mrs Cummings had never liked.

Many people had described Albert as looking and behaving like an ill tempered bulldog, so perhaps the violence was no surprise to some as Baker had told Corner off on several occasions and threatened him with the sack if he didn't improve his behaviour. Matters came to such a head on the Friday after dinner, while Baker was busy shearing sheep. Albert was lounging against the gate watching him, probably with a straw hanging out of the corner of his mouth and a sneer on his face.

Hubert had looked rather pointedly at his watch, saying, 'It's five to two and time you went after the horses'.

Albert uttered a mouthful of filthy language, snatched up a crowbar and threatened to 'flatten' Hubert with it. Fortunately when the latter made no effort to retaliate, he cooled down, realising he had gone too far, but Baker told him it was the last straw and he would have to go at the end of the month.

Hubert had related the details of this encounter to his sister, Mrs Cummings, and she suggested he did not wait for the end of the month, but pay him off at once. As always, he took her advice and paid him on the Saturday afternoon. Albert went up to his room and packed his belongings after tea.

While his sister was milking, Hubert took some cows out to the field and young Wilfred Perrott went with him, which was often the case as the two families were good neighbours. It was as they crossed the field that the boy had called out, pointing at the hedge, 'There's Albert with a gun!'

Baker, who had had his back to the boy, swung round to look in the direction he was pointing. Before he could take any evasive action Albert Corner fired from a range of only a few yards, striking Baker in the face. He fell to the ground but somehow, although it was a miracle he could do so, he managed to get to his feet calling out to his sister . . . 'Annie! Oh, oh!'

He then started to run down the hill with Albert racing after him. Firing again he hit Baker in the shoulder, and instantly the man fell to the ground – mortally wounded.

The boy was uninjured and it is difficult to imagine what on earth his feelings must have been, but he ran through the gate to fetch Mrs Cummings and by the Grace of God Albert took no notice of him.

She had heard the two shots and had already run to the stable, where two men were attending to the horses.

An artist's impression of Warcombe Farm, where Hubert Baker died.

'I heard a couple of shots, go and see what is happening.'

As they reached the scene, at first they thought there had been an accident then one of them caught sight of Albert and, climbing on the hedge, shouted at him that he had killed the 'maister'.

There was no reply but there were two more shots. Hurrying back to where Hubert lay the two men put his body on a hurdle. Then one of them went to fetch the police.

They found Albert in the next field with his face blown off, the gun between his legs, the muzzle pointing to the centre of his head. In his right hand was a stick which he had obviously torn from the hedge, with which to fire the trigger. A few yards away was his tin box which held his possessions – the gun beside him was Hubert's.

Mrs Cummings, badly shocked, said that earlier, when she was milking, her brother had come to see her in the shippon as he went to the field to see to the bullocks. He had told her, 'It's all right now, Albert is gone and his box with him so you need not be afraid any more'.

The gun had been in the larder in its usual place on Saturday afternoon, she knew that because she had had to move it to wash the floor. Albert must have slipped in after he left the house with his box while she was in the shippon, and picked up the gun and cartridges.

As she said this, Albert's father protested that the gun and cartridges had been left within easy reach, lying about, despite frequent cases of men who in a fit of temper had been known to destroy either themselves or others. At that time this was a quite extraordinary remark to make, for there would hardly have been a farm in Devon that did not have a shotgun and cartridges within easy access for destroying vermin and killing rabbits for the pot.

The verdict was that Albert Corner was guilty of wilful murder and then committed suicide, being of sound mind at the time. As a murderer and suicide he was buried by lamplight at West Alvington church at 10 pm by the vicar, the Rev. T. Bell-Salter. A grave had been prepared at the head of the churchyard under a tree close to the hedge – presumably this was considered ground suitable for such a criminal. Mr Mundy, the Relieving Officer, had made the arrangements for this as Corner's parents refused to accept responsibility.

Is it possible to say they were responsible or not for the boy to whom they had given life, or for the way he shaped that life from the day he was born?

THE FETCH

Ihad been invited to open the Folk Music Festival at South Zeal, which meant standing on an extremely rickety hay wain and shouting against the wind while everyone, justifiably, wanted to get on with the gorgeous music. The breeze apart, the sun was warm as was the enthusiasm but it was pleasant later to go to the nearby Oxenham Arms for a pint or two of local cider and a pasty. We consumed this in the small bar behind the main one wherein stands the mystical granite monolith which it seems goes down through the ground probably as far as 'Oz' for all we know for in spite of many people trying to find its base no one has succeeded. It seems the monks had built what was then their rest house round it while they also built the church. At one time this building was a Dower House for the Oxenham family and these were the people who were pestered by a 'Fetch' or personification leading to the mysterious story of the White Bird of the Oxenhams.

The village of South Tawton stands at the foot of Cosdon, the huge hill that seems to dominate the north east corner of Dartmoor. Just beyond this is Oxenham which takes its name from the family whose seat was Oxenham Manor at Zeal Monachorum.

The tradition of this pesky bird which has lasted down the centuries to almost the present day is that when the head of the family or, in some cases, another member is about to die, this white breasted bird will hover above them. The first description of this bird appeared in print in 1611. Later it was said to have been seen flying over members of James Oxenham's family. In 1635 his eldest son John aged 22 and a strong, healthy, well set up chap, died suddenly for no apparent reason. Two days before his death two people had told both the Vicar and the Bishop that they had seen this phenomenon.

The next victim was Thomazine, John's sister-in-law, then her sister Rebecca aged only eight. Next on the list was the baby son of James and Thomazine who died in his cradle as the bird flew over him.

At first it was thought they might be victims of the plague but apparently there were no symptoms of that disease.

According to the illustration in my book of birds, an ouzel – which this is said to be – is much like a thrush with a white breast and it is the white breast which is mentioned particularly by anyone who sees it.

James Howell in *Familiar Letters*, 1645, records that in 1632 he saw, in a stonecutter's shop in London, a 'memorial tablet' on which was engraved details of the bird's appearance to members of the family. The tablet had been intended for a burial in Exeter but it never arrived.

In a commonplace book found at Oxenham Manor in South Zeal, there is a ballad about the bird. It tells of a Sir James Oxenham who had a beautiful daughter named Margaret who was not only beautiful but kind and loving, the apple of his eye. Naturally she was wooed by all the local young men, amongst these was one who had not been favoured with her reciprocation to his passion. When he found she had become betrothed to someone else he swore he would have his revenge, if he could not have her then nor should anyone else. This is a resolution which seems to have been very popular in those days as recounted in R. D. Blackmore's famous *Lorna Doone*.

The Oxenham Arms at South Zeal.

It was Christmas Eve, Sir James was giving an enormous banquet and other jollifications for everyone in the area – Margaret was to marry on Boxing Day.

Her father was delighted with the young man his daughter had chosen although he would miss her, but he rose to his feet while the people ate, trying to put into words all the love he had for this wonderful girl. He even spoke of his future son in law as if he were his own son.

The diners listened with much interest but were a little surprised as suddenly James appeared to falter in his speech. He sank back in his chair, knocking over the glass of scarlet wine which spread on the white cloth like blood. Perhaps the whole emotion of the scene had been too much for him. However, it was nothing so happy for he had seen the cursed white bird which had flown high above the table and had circled once round Margaret. He knew only too well what it foretold.

On Boxing Day the church of South Tawton was filled to the doors with people to watch Margaret as she walked up the aisle to join her lover at the altar. The parson began the service, he had only spoken the opening words when from behind a pillar a man sprang forward and plunged a dagger into Margaret's breast. Before anyone could move, for they had all been paralysed with shock, the young man withdrew the dagger from Margaret as the scarlet blood spurted out, and plunged it into his own heart. True to his threat the rejected suitor had carried it out. Probably with all this drama no one noticed – except Sir James – the white bird hovering above the body of his beloved daughter as his foreboding was fulfilled.

Many members of the family said the whole thing was rubbish. In 1743 the bird appeared to William Oxenham, but he was one of the kind who treated the whole thing as a fabrication of his ancestors who had probably looked upon the wine once too often. He firmly refused to believe its appearance was any kind of an omen. In any case he was perfectly healthy – it was just an ordinary thrush which had got caught in a bush or something – the whole thing would turn out to be a complete fabrication. Several days later he died.

There were more reported sightings in 1810 and 1821; the latter in Sidmouth when those who were attending a sick Oxenham man on his death bed saw a white bird flying round the room. It seemed to hover over the man and then disappeared into an open cupboard. History does not relate if it flew out again!

More up to date was the sighting before the death in 1873 of Mr G. N. Oxenham in Kensington. His nephew, the Reverend Henry Oxenham, said he had seen a white bird fluttering outside the window. It was no bigger than a pigeon, it beat against the window pane and then perched on a bush in the garden. He summoned some men to catch it but it eluded them.

Theo Brown told me that in the late 1960s she had spoken to an elderly lady who was an Oxenham. However, she was one who definitely looked upon the whole thing as a made up story and said anyone who believed it was ridiculous though her uncle said he had seen a white bird on the edge of Exmoor in 1919 when her mother, his sister, was dying.

Another well known writer, Sarah Hewett, said a member of the family who wished to remain anonymous had told her the bird had appeared to him in 1892 very soon after his father had died. There are even rumours that the bird had materialised in Canada where it had appeared at the death of a member of the family who had emigrated.

So, what is the truth about this feathered creature which has made the family's life and death so miserable and mysterious for so many centuries? Other examples of these appearances can be found in family histories in Devon where they are known as Projections or Fetches but usually in the form of black dogs, foxes, hares, rather than as in this case, a bird.

There are about half a dozen Oxenhams in the telephone directory. At random I picked the one who lived nearest to me – William Oxenham of Bovey Tracey. He told me he himself had been born in Cornwall and had only heard vaguely of the curse but was inclined to agree with those of the family who regarded the whole thing as an interesting but rather far fetched (!) legend when perhaps some of the Oxenhams had been looking on the wine when it was rather highly coloured!

Be that as it may there is no harm in believing that there are more things in heaven and earth. . .

THINGS THAT GO BUMP IN NORTH DEVON

DRIVING through Mid Devon to the north of the county the country is somehow secretive, with great Saxon earth banks behind which the lush meadows lie in soft folds and the names of parishes and hundreds tell of the age of the communities. This is a journey to Frithelstock, turning west at Bideford along the A39 for a brief visit to Clovelly, retracing our steps to Abbotsham and ending at Appledore where I had read of a haunted vicarage. All four visits are brief but none the less mysterious and rewarding.

The ruined priory of Frithelstock near Great Torrington achieved a certain notoriety in 1351 when it was reported to the Bishop of Exeter that the monks had built a chapel in the woods outside the village. This contained a strange statue which the prior said was of Our Lady. The bishop, who was probably a bit miffed because no one had asked his permission, said it sounded to him more like 'proud and disobedient Eve or unchaste Diana', and ordered it to be removed at once and the chapel which had held it to be demolished.

Eventually the storm in a teacup died down and the priory resumed its normal state of grace until the Reformation in 1536 when it was surrendered to the king. The priory church crumbled slowly so all that remains are the walls and a few arches of the old priory next to the parish church.

Frithelstock Priory and parish church.

These remains were excavated in 1932. Before this started a member of the committee went over to examine the ruins to plan how it should be done. With her went her daughter and grandson Christopher aged seven. This is how she told the story to Theo Brown, who kindly passed it on to me.

They parked the car in the road and walked to the church down the path along the south wall, to a small wicket gate at the east end.

Christopher ran on ahead as children do, and it took the two ladies a little while to catch up with him. He had stopped and was standing just inside the gate calling out, 'Oh how lovely! I'm so glad we came. I love this place. . .'

His grandmother smiled and said, 'You've never been here before and neither has your mother, that is why I brought you both to see it.'

The child looked at his gran and said with great emphasis for one so young, 'I HAVE been here before, I have, I have! Long ago when I was a very old man.'

Before the women could get over their astonishment he ran to the west end of the ruin by the east end of the church, where again he cried out, 'Oh, what have they done to my lovely tower – my lovely tower which went up windey up to where I pulled the bell.' As he spoke he was climbing a steep grass-grown heap and stood looking up into the sky.

'And the roof! Where's that gone?'

It was his mother's turn; she said quite sharply, 'You've never been here before, Christopher.' But there was no mistaking the puzzled, disappointed look on his face, he seemed quite bewildered.

His gran asked gently, 'When were you here?'

'Oh, long, long ago, I rang the bell. It was before I went to sleep. . . Oh, my lovely tower!'

He stood there for a few seconds, then as if nothing had happened, no words had been spoken, he began to play among the stones and ruins like any small boy would.

No tower was shown on any of the old plans and if you think about it this would be the last feature you would expect to find sandwiched between the south wall of a priory and the east end of a parish church.

But when the excavation started that is exactly what they did find. It is shown on the plan in the Report of the Proceedings of the Devon Archaeological Exploration Society vol.ii plate VI.

Can we sometimes actually see something that has happened in the past recorded on some timeless kind of cinematography, an impression perhaps of violence or evil left after some such deed, or perhaps a happy memory as the child had? Who can say?

When I was a child, I often heard my grandmother who was born at Ide near Exeter, talking of something being a 'lot of gubbins!' I discovered in the dictionary that this means 'trash, valueless thing, foolish person', so it was no surprise it probably came from the name Gubbings, a gang who in the 16th century were a sinister threat around Lydford, layabouts who stole from and terrified their neighbours. Their counterparts were the Grieffs who lived in a cave in Clovelly for 25 years.

John Grieff with his wife, eight sons and one daughter, 18 granddaughters and 14 grandsons robbed, murdered, and were actually said to have eaten, a thousand local people.

Eventually the locals could stand it no longer and 400 men and a pack of bloodhounds rounded up this gruesome gang. They took them to Plymouth where the men were dismembered in front of the women – identical treatment to that they had meted out to others. Any who survived were burned to death.

Clovelly – as it was!

There are many versions of this story, so perhaps it was an invention put about by smugglers in the Clovelly area to keep nosey folk away from the barrels stored in the cave. Just a thought.

Time to move on to Appledore for the culmination of our visit to this area, but on the way through Abbotsham I decided to call in at Thatched House, a lovely 300 year old pub and like so many, with its own ghost. In this case a rather unusual one, as it is a taxi-driver.

Bob Marsh and his wife were running the pub in those days and according to the villagers this taxi driver had been a regular customer who had died mysteriously many years ago having driven his car – or been pushed – over a nearby cliff. Rumours were rife of some kind of love affair on the side; it was known he was married. Bob said the haunting was just the usual sounds in such cases – footsteps on the stairs, glasses clinking, bottles being moved around when the

The Thatched Inn, Abbotsham, is haunted by a taxi driver.

bar was closed and empty. No one had actually seen anything, unless you could count the dog whose fur often stood on end as he came crashing down the stairs, while Bob's mother who lived with them flatly refused to sleep upstairs.

The haunting was a little unusual however, as it involved a glass of advocaat being left in the bedroom on the man's birthday – it was his favourite drink. Was this where the rendezvous with his love took place? Anyway, the contents of the glass had always disappeared by morning.

Bob's wife, June, didn't seem to be bothered by it but she said that the sounds and other odd things that had happened when china ornaments and so on were moved around were too frequent to be imagination.

Today Les Heard is the landlord and he told me, 'I have heard odd noises in the bar when I have been upstairs and the bar not yet open'. He paused a moment when I mentioned the advocaat. 'I do have to admit we have given up leaving that about because it went bad, trouble is I haven't a clue when the chap's birthday is – and he hasn't let me know – yet!'

Finally to Appledore and that haunted vicarage that I had read about. Mrs Anne MacLeod Crisp had very kindly answered the letter I wrote having seen the piece in the newspaper. She and her husband John, who had retired from the Metropolitan Police after 31 years, were busy renovating The Old Vicarage; it dates back to 1901 and had 13 fireplaces but no modern conveniences!

In April 1984 John had to go to London for a week. After listening to the ten o'clock news on the radio Anne turned it off and went up to bed in the room known as the Blue and Orange Room; it was the guest room as their own was in the chaos of decoration. The room had bars at the window as though children had once used it. At 2 am she was woken by the sound of the radio playing very loudly downstairs, but

The Old Vicarage at Appledore.

she was certain she had turned it off. As she got out of bed it stopped. Even modern technology does not usually turn a radio on and off unless set to do so.

She dialled 999 from the phone by her bed. When the police arrived they searched the house and garden, but there was nothing and no sign of entry. She apologised profusely on bringing them out but explained that she was on her own – they replied it was just part of the night's work and no doubt appreciated the cups of hot coffee at that time in the morning. Feeling reassured Anne went back to bed.

At 4 am she woke again with a kind of buzzing in her ears. Two little girls were standing by the bed laughing, teasing her as if they knew she had sent for the police. She put out her hand and they simply vanished, but their looks were imprinted on her mind. They were about eight or nine years old with long blonde hair and dressed in Victorian style with little lace collars rather like Alice in Wonderland.

A few days later Anne's stepson, Richard came to stay. Next morning he asked her if there had ever been a Rev. Muller living in the house. Rather surprised, Anne said actually the incumbent before the last two had been named Muller. He had a wooden leg, or a limp of some kind.

Richard said he had heard someone walking in exactly that style, with difficulty, and a voice had called out, 'Good night, Reverend Muller.'

It was impossible for Richard to have heard about this in the village as he had only just arrived.

Anne took me into the room where she had seen the little girls. I took a photo of her on the bed but although the rest of the spool came out perfectly, that one was blank. She then took me into the room which the vicars down the years had used as a study to write their sermons. I said, 'I like the perfume of your spray – it's like incense.'

She smiled, 'Many people say the same thing, but there's no spray. . .'

When I was talking to a vicar about this he said he was not at all surprised the departed should pick vicarages to return to, as they are peaceful places and a spiritual refuge.

So there we are – from a strange echo of the past to the timeless peace of a vicarage, with cannibals and an unfaithful taxi driver sandwiched between, in this beautiful, unspoilt part of the county.

MYSTERIES BEYOND THE GRAVE

JAY'S Grave is one of the most famous of Dartmoor's landmarks and has a strange history.

In 1860 a roadman was cleaning out the gutters and ditches near Hound Tor when his spade caught in something hard in the middle of a rough mound. Managing to separate this from the roots and stones, he found a piece of bone. He was about to fling it on one side as part of some moorland animal which had died when he looked down and saw more bones which were unmistakably from a human hand.

Eventually a complete skeleton was unearthed and taken to Squire Bryant's nearby home at Hedge Barton. It so happened that at the time he had a doctor friend visiting him. He examined the bones and said they were of a female human, probably quite young.

The squire had a coffin brought and the bones laid inside, burying it where it had been found under a small mound. Many years later in 1970 the Dartmoor National Park Authority had a kerb placed round to protect it from cattle. This strange position for the grave, where three parishes meet, was because in those days the intolerance of society denied a suicide victim burial on hallowed ground.

Whilst researching the background to this story I decided I could do no better than quote the words of Beatrice Chase, The Lady of the Moor, particularly as one of the only other references I could find of any authenticity was from William Crossing who described the grave as 'this pathetic little mound'. Beatrice wrote, 'The grave is that of poor little Mary Jay, an orphan apprentice from Newton Abbot Workhouse about the same period that Dickens was writing of Oliver Twist. Her name is on the Apprentices Register, long discarded, which was in the possession of the retired Guardian. At the age of 15 she was apprenticed to a farmer at Canna Farm near Wingstone and in due course took a rope and hanged herself in a barn.'

It seems that Mary Jay (also known as Kitty Jay) had been seduced by the son of the farmer and when she found she was pregnant she hanged herself, for in those days single mothers were not treated with the same relaxed attitude as they are today. Her body was then buried in that lonely grave.

Beatrice continues: 'The agony of mind, the utter friendlessness of that poor child does not bear contemplating, all the kindness and sympathy came too late. I have known the grave for over 40 years and never even during two world wars have I seen it without some kind of rough decoration. Who puts these there we have never discovered. Sometimes it is only a few sprigs of laurel, one summer it was a bridal bouquet. On the first Armistice Day I put one of the little wooden crosses with a poppy in the centre and the one word, Remembrance. Next Armistice Day there were scores of such crosses. The grave was a sheet of scarlet. If only the poor child could have seen this sympathy. As it is we can only accept the warning never to withhold pity and help.'

The most mysterious part about this grave is the perpetual and rather eerie placing of these floral decorations. For three decades I have been in that part of the moor in different seasons and weather conditions and I have never seen it without some kind of offering, from berries and leaves to roses and carnations.

Kitty Jay's grave.

There are other legends connected with the grave, for instance from gypsies who say the land is cursed because of her tragic death and they will never pitch their camp nearby for fear of bad luck. Others say that on a moonlit night a dark figure can be seen kneeling at the site heavily muffled in cloak and hood, perhaps Kitty herself, or is it her lover keeping vigil eternally over the spot where this girl and his unborn child are buried. Even coins are found on the grave which gives it almost wishing well status.

Another grave of interest – among many – is away from the moor itself, but this is of Squire Cabell on whom Conan Doyle based his tale of *The Hound of the Baskervilles*. He was the man who had apparently sold his soul to the Devil and whose ghost rides the moor accompanied by a pack of black hell-hounds.

The wicked Sir Henry Baskerville was said to be based on Squire Richard Cabell of Brook Manor near Buckfastleigh in the 17th century. Believing his wife to be unfaithful he drove her out of the house and as she fled across the moor he caught up with her and stabbed her to death, but her faithful hound turned on him and tore out his throat. This ghastly hound was said to prowl Dartmoor and reappear to frighten the living daylights out of each succeeding generation, slavering at the mouth as it claimed its victim. The other story is that he had an evil reputation for seducing innocent maids and persecuting the Nonconformists – a popular pastime for many years – and for threatening to foreclose on mortgages. However, there is said to be evidence that actually Squire Cabell's wife survived him by 14 years and that he was really a mild and kind man. As none of us were alive at the time it is best, as they say, to pay your money and take your choice.

Squire Cabell's tomb at Buckfastleigh.

What we do know is that in his will Cabell left a clause to the effect that unless an enormous and most ornate tomb was built for him in the churchyard at Buckfastleigh he would come back to haunt the local people, accompanied by the Devil. The grave is perfectly preserved and visited by people from all over the world, particularly the USA where some families claim relationship with him. But beware, for the Devil is waiting behind the bars to seize any hands which are thrust inside. During the Second World War feelings ran high when it was suggested that the railings be removed in the collection of metal for the manufacture of Spitfires. The local people put up such firm opposition that the plan had to be abandoned.

It is said you can always find one quotation to contradict another. Edmund Burke said, 'Superstition is the religion of feeble minds,' but Goethe, 'Superstition is the poetry of life.' The choice is yours. Whatever we choose to believe about this legend, the retelling of it has brought immense pleasure and interest to tens of thousands of people and surely there is no harm in that.

SURELY THE DEVIL MUST THEM POSSESS

O N the north-west coast of Devon lies Hartland Point, to the north is Hartland Quay and inland, completing the triangle, is Hartland town. The residents are mainly typical friendly Devonians, but this community has known some horrible tales of murder and mayhem.

The Quay itself goes back before the time of Queen Elizabeth I. Because of the remoteness of the parish and the difficulties of travel overland in those days, the port was Hartland's key to the commerce of the outside world for nearly three centuries. The daily life of many of the residents was frequently spiced by war, wrecks and tempest. Now it is a favourite haunt of locals and sightseers from round the world. The coastal scenery is breathtaking, and people are drawn by its most precarious position, a kind of toehold between the cliffs and the encroaching sea.

Trade in the 17th and 18th centuries varied from lead for roofing in Bristol, lime for the building trade and coal from across the Bristol Channel, to corn. And with two of its boundaries flanked north and west by open sea, Hartland's involvement in the fishing industry is as certain as that of Clovelly's. Daniel Defoe connected Hartland with this in 1724 when he described 'the great gainful fishing trade carried on for herrings on this coast.'

However, two men who frequented this area were

The Quay buildings in the 1920s. (By kind permission of Hartland Quay Museum)

certainly not those one would choose as neighbours. One was Peter Vine, who was born in Hartland of very respectable and God-fearing parents. Peter had leanings towards the Church so it was no surprise when he announced that he wanted to enter the ministry. He duly received Holy Orders and was made the vicar of his home town, Hartland. He was well respected and seemed to be the ideal vicar, paying home calls on his parishioners and educating the children of both the wealthy and the poor.

One of the homes which he visited regularly was that of a Mrs Dark, who lived in a beautiful house with a large garden. He was teaching her eleven year old daughter. On a pleasant afternoon in January 1811, he was walking in the garden with his pupil and her mother. Mrs Dark was called back into the house to speak to a visitor, leaving her daughter in the trusted company of the priest. While she was gone, Vine attacked the girl and raped her, leaving her lying on the ground. He then leapt over the low wall and vanished.

When her mother returned and saw what had happened she fainted at the sight which met her eyes. A servant came to find Mrs Dark, wondering why she and her daughter had not returned to the house. On seeing the two prostrate figures she rushed for help. An immediate search was made, and Mrs Dark offered 20 guineas to anyone who could provide information leading to the arrest of Vine.

One can imagine the horror, disgust and surprise in the neighbourhood at the terrible crime, but the months passed and there was no sign of the man.

Then on a 17th April of the same year, Vine returned to Hartland brandishing a gun and saying he would shoot anyone who attempted to arrest him. With perfect calm he simply returned to his home.

By now rumours were rife that he was possessed of the devil – and also a shotgun. Nothing daunted, Mrs Dark obtained a warrant for his arrest. Three constables went to his house, which was well fortified with bars across the door. However, they managed to gain entry and one of them, a man called Ashton, then broke down the locked door to face Vine, who immediately shot him dead. The other two managed to disarm the priest, who was taken to the cells and in due course appeared before a Justice of the Peace.

Vine would not confess to the rape of Mrs Dark's daughter although it was pointed out that his immediate disappearance made him look extremely guilty. Calmly he explained this away by the fact that he had suddenly had news that his father was very ill. This seems extraordinary – how did he imagine they would think he could have received a message without anyone seeing the carrier of the news?

However, he had no defence for the shooting of the man Ashton and on 25th April 1811, in spite of his protestations, he was found guilty of murder and also of raping a child. He was sentenced to death by hanging on 4th May 1811.

During his imprisonment Vine seemed to revert to his original character, praying with the other prisoners and gaining much respect from the warders. He also had a favourite prayer which he repeated aloud over and over again, seeking God's mercy as he repented of his sins.

When he reached the place of execution and climbed the steps to the gallows, it was as if the priest was ascending to his pulpit one more time. He preached to the assembled people, claiming to be not guilty of rape, and that the killing of Ashton had been in self defence. However, those watching did not swallow the excuse that he had absconded because of the illness of his father. Naturally his crimes created much local interest, and verses were written about him:

> Surely the Devil must him possess,
> For to commit such wickedness,
> On her he did commit rape,
> And left her in a shocking state.

Hardly worthy of Shakespeare but in the last verse holds good advice:

> Now he's executed for the same,
> Great numbers went to see him die in shame,
> By this minister's fate be warned I pray,
> Never let your passions lead you astray.

The other evil character who concerns us here was known as Cruel Coppinger (sometimes spelt Copinger) – a pirate, wrecker and smuggler who flourished in the 18th century. His story has a basis of truth which has increased in interest

Hartland Pier, from an aquatint by William Daniell RA (1769–1837). (By kind permission of Hartland Quay Museum)

down the years. One of the writers who told his story was parson Steven Hawker of Morwenstow. He describes Coppinger's arrival in the area amidst a terrible hurricane: 'a strange vessel of foreign rig was seen struggling through the enormous waves. As it neared the shore it lost its battle with the billows and the huge figure of a man could be seen standing on board the heaving vessel, naked, as he threw his clothes on one side, plunged into the buffeting waves and powered his way to the surf, reaching the shore with one bound. An old woman stood among the crowd, he seized her cloak and wrapping it round himself, leapt on to the back of a white horse upon which a young girl was sitting. Kicking his heels on its flanks, the horse galloped off.'

This man washed up on Welcombe Mouth was none other than Coppinger the Dane and he made the girl, Dinah

Hamlyn, take him to her father's house at Galsham. He married her and as soon as her father died his evil character became evident. His gang of desperadoes created every kind of uproar in the quiet neighbourhood but nobody dared cross him; one Revenue man who did was decapitated over the gunwhale of his own ship. Coppinger's cave six miles south of Hartland Point at Gull Rock was the site for wild carousing with food from sheep and cattle stolen, drink of brandy, gin, port and sherry smuggled, and 'doxies' also imported from France cavorting in lace and silk. Meanwhile his wife at Galsham was having his baby, which proved to be a deaf mute who grew up to be a brute like his father, throwing his playmate over the cliff and smiling happily at the broken body on the rocks below.

Coppinger carried on smuggling, privateering, whipping anyone who dared ask for money he owed, beating his wife, swearing and whoring, all unchecked. Some men he took on board his favourite schooner, the *Black Prince*, were made to swear allegiance to the marauding crew. Gold flowed into his hands from across the world, and when he went to buy a farm he would appear before the astonished lawyer handling the sale with bags filled with every kind of coin – dollars, ducats, doubloons, pistoles and guineas from any foreign country with a seaboard.

It seemed no one could touch him, he even hijacked the lanes and byways and the cliff paths for his own use. Having squandered his wife's money, he would have done the same with that of his mother in law if she had not hidden it, whereupon he tied his wife to the bedpost and with a cat-o'-nine-tails in one hand threatened to beat her while her mother watched unless she handed over her money and jewels – which of course she did.

At one time it was rumoured the king's men were getting too close for comfort and at last there was a showdown and many on both sides were killed.

It was time for Coppinger to disappear. During another turbulent storm such as the one when he had arrived, the burly figure leapt into a boat, his sword flashing. The oarsmen strained to cut through the thundering waves and land him back on his own ship. It was out of sight in a moment, pursued by thunder, lightning and hail. Trees were rent up by the roots around his house where his wife awaited him and, as if to say goodbye in the style to which he was accustomed, a boulder whipped up by the storm fell through the roof, to land at the very feet of his vacant chair. Did he get his comeuppance? Not, as far as we know, in this world.

There are so many versions of this extraordinary story – some saying the whole thing is a legend, while others can produce proof such a man did exist – that we are spoiled for choice in trying to separate the wheat from the chaff.

There is little doubt there is a basis of truth about some such character but from whence he came, whether Denmark or Ireland, no one knows. Certainly he was not a man to meet on a dark night. Some facts have been produced that a man was wrecked at Marsland Mouth in December 1792 called Daniel Herbert Copinger, who did marry a Miss Hamlyn of Galsham – but she was named Ann not Dinah and was aged 42. She died before he did and was buried in Hartland churchyard.

Baring-Gould suggests Coppinger was a highly successful smugglers' merchant who may well have indulged in smuggling himself. That Daniel Copinger was an officer in the Royal Navy – was he an officer and a smuggler? Was 'Cruel Coppinger' deliberately given publicity to keep eyes away from the caves containing contraband, as in the case of the Grieffs of Clovelly? The story poses more questions than it answers.

In his *History of the Royal Navy*, Captain Brenton writes of smugglers who when caught (usually acting against the Revenue Laws) were sent out on ships of war as a punishment: 'these men are hardy, sober, faithful to each other beyond the generality of seamen and when shipwreck occurs have been known to perform deeds not exceeded in any country in the world, unequalled in the annals of other maritime powers.' In other words, the Royal Navy found smugglers much better seamen than the usual run of men rounded up by the Press Gangs – and they gained rapid promotion!

So once again an unsolved mystery, which is best read and enjoyed simply for the story it tells.